Swimming the River of Stone

Praise for *Swimming the River of Stone*

"The sheer grace and power of the language amazes me."
— Annie Dillard, *Pilgrim at Tinker Creek*

"Ayres is an artist of the human spirit."
— Ilia Delio, OSF, *The Unbearable Wholeness of Being*

"The imagery — deep as the sea, high as the sky — reveals the immensity of our inner world yet remains firmly rooted in daily life."
— Karen Karper Fredette, *Consider the Ravens*

"Elizabeth Ayres is Claude Monet with words."
— Paula Cohen, *Gramercy Park*

Also by Elizabeth Ayres

Home After Exile:
A Spiritual Odyssey

Mirror of Our Becoming:
Meditations on Nature's Beauty, Wisdom and Mystery

Writing the Wave:
Inspired Rides for Aspiring Writers

Creative Writing from A to Z
(audio book series)

Invitation to Wonder 'Journey' Series
(audio books)

For information on these titles please visit

www.CreativeWritingCenter.com

Swimming the River of Stone

COLLECTED POEMS

ELIZABETH AYRES

Veriditas Books

Copyright © 2014 by Elizabeth Ayres

Published by Veriditas Books
P. O. Box 968 • California, MD 20619
1-800-510-1049
VeriditasBooks.com • info@veriditasbooks.com

All rights reserved. No part of this book may be reproduced, stored in a retrieval system, or transmitted by any means, electronic, mechanical, photocopying, recording, or otherwise, without written permission from the author.

ISBN 13: 978-0-9845178-9-3
ISBN 10: 0-9845178-9-8
Library of Congress Control Number: 2014934715

Cover Design by Karen Phillips (www.phillipscovers.com)
Musical Notation by Mac Ritchey (www.possumhall.com)

"First Female Astronaut" first published by *Van Gogh's Ear*, Volume 4, 2005; "Circus Family" first published by *The Worcester Review*, Vol. XIX, nos. 1 and 2, 1998; *Poems from the Noh* excerpted in *The Malahat Review*, No. 55, 1980.

Poems from the Noh is a collection of found poems from *The Classic Noh Theater of Japan* by Ezra Pound and Ernest Fenollosa (New Directions, 1979). Use of the original text adheres to section two of American University's Center for Social Media's "Code of Best Uses in Fair Use for Poetry," which states, in part: "A poet may make use of quotations from existing poetry, literary prose, and non-literary material, if these quotations are re-presented in poetic forms that add value through significant imaginative or intellectual transformation, whether direct or (as in the case of poetry-generating software) indirect."

for
all the swimmers

because
it's the one, necessary thing

"A mystery is not something that is unknowable.
It's something that is infinitely knowable."
– Richard Rohr, OFM

Contents

Introduction 1

Book One
Why We Do It

The Dance 14
Black Magic 16
Dragon Dream 19
The Orphan 25
Thoughts for a New Decade 28
An Artist's Prayer 30
Circus Family 32
The Seventh Wave 35
New Day Dawning 39
Wealth 41
Swimming the River of Stone 43
Why We Do It 48

Book Two
Portraits from the Dreamtime

Woman in a Man's World 52
First Female Astronaut 55
The Gardener 60

Book Three
The Owl & The Stallion

The Owl & The Stallion 74

Book Four
Poems from the Noh

Preface 94
Kinuta (I) 98
Kayoi Kamachi (I) 99
Kumasaka 100
Sotoba Komachi 101
Shojo 102
Kayoi Kamachi (II) 103
Hagomoro (I) 104
Suma Genji (I) 105
Kinuta (II) 106
Niskikigi (I) 107
Tamura 108
Kinuta (III) 109
Awoi No Uye 110
Niskikigi (II) 111
Chorio 112
Kakitsubata 113
Niskikigi (III) 114
Niskikigi (IV) 115
Tsunemasa (I) 116
Suma Genji (II) 117
Kagekiyo (I) 118
Kagekiyo (II) 119
Genjo 120
Hagomoro (II) 121
Tsunemasa (II) 122

Book Five
Songs from Silence

Eucharist	124
Baptism	126
Passing Through	129
Learning to Live as One	131
Grave-Song	133
Fire Flowers	135
For Richard, on Graduation Day	136
God Speaks from Within Your Heart	138

Book Six
Beckonings

"Behind the walls of my eyes"	142, 143
"One by one they vanish"	144, 145
"Here is where words lose their meaning"	146, 147
"And if you wanted to remember"	148, 149
"The Word became Flesh"	150, 151
"Oh Lady, most pure"	152, 153
"Sunlight and shadow divide the world"	154, 155
"Lord, I have no other desire"	156, 157

Book Seven
Psalms for a New Millennium

Psalm 151	160
Psalm 152	161
Psalm 153	162
Psalm 154	163
Psalm 155	164
Psalm 156	165
Psalm 157	167
Psalm 158	168

Psalm 159 169
Psalm 160 170
Psalm 161 171

BOOK EIGHT
Moments Out of Time

The Mindfulness Bell 174
Little Blind Bird 175
The Dream of Spiders 176
The Gift 177
Possibilities 178
Water Skies 179
Seed Heads 180
The Amish Woman at Wal-Mart 181
While I Wait 182
Wisdom 183
A Contemplative's Lexicon 184
Discovery 185
Illumination 186
Autumn 187
9/11/13 188
Sunny Morning on Herring Creek 190
Life Lesson 191
How Poetry Works 192
September Morning (I) 193
September Morning (II) 194
Flight 195
Dawn 196
Caffeine and Contemplation 197
Snipping Flowers for William 198
When Ellen Meditates 199
Moment Out of Time 200
Secret Birth 201

Book Nine
The Raven Chronicles

Raven Gazes into the Fire 204
Raven Fights the Wind..205
Raven Discusses Politics 206
Raven the Omnivore 207
Raven Longs for God 208
Raven Praises the Color Black 209
Raven Mourns the Start of Yet Another War.......................210
Passing Over Our Lady of the Desert Monastery,
    Raven Shares a Thought About Discipline....................211
Raven Spots Ton Haak Hiking in Windmill Cove
    on His 60th Birthday 212
Raven Spouts Some Theology...213
Raven Complains About Living Hand to Mouth.................214
Raven Describes the Heart of God 215
Raven Bears Witness to the Resurrection of Jesus Christ.....216
Raven Becomes the Notes to a Song.....................................217

    A Message from the Author 219
    Also by Elizabeth Ayres 222-225
    Acknowledgements...227
    About the Author 229

Introduction

As I write, a polar vortex has descended on the eastern United States, plunging Maryland's Chesapeake Bay landscape into the frigid days and nights typical of my childhood. Back then, winter meant ice-skating on our frozen creeks and rivers; more recently, global warming has put an end to such sport. This winter, however, climate change has hijacked arctic air currents, dumping Alaska's weather on Georgia and leaving both north and south exposed to dangerously atypical temperatures.

This morning a flock of crows strutted on ice-clad Herring Creek. While I don't profess any magical insight into the workings of the corvine mind, I am certain those birds – their black feathers consuming color the way black holes gobble gravity – were excited. Suddenly, unaccountably, they have been given the opportunity to achieve the impossible. This morning those crows walked on water.

Every human heart longs to achieve the impossible. We desire the good, the beautiful, the true. We're confronted by the bad, the ugly, the false. Still it beckons, our heart's desire, urging us to do the impossible, to resolve the paradox, to find the reality hidden beneath appearance: to swim a river of stone.

We have many names for our destination: goodness, beauty, truth, love, nirvana, God. The writer-monk Thomas Merton, harking back to early Sufi sources, calls it "le point vierge," or "the virgin point." He says, "At the center of our being is a point of nothingness which is untouched by sin and by illusion, a point of pure truth, a point or spark which belongs entirely to God, which is never at our disposal, from which God disposes of our lives, which is inaccessible to the fantasies of our mind or the brutalities of our own will. This little point of nothingness and of absolute poverty is the pure glory of God in us."

I am a poet. Over a lifetime, I have used images – and the musicality of the words that evoke those images – to search for *le point vierge*. In the poem "Black Magic," for instance, I write, "Last night I dreamt I was removing/scarf after colored scarf from between us. Each one/became its own story, and told itself/in its own language until there was nothing left of any of them/except a low hum." I think that 'low hum' and Merton's 'divine spark' are one and the same thing, I can't be sure, but I am certain that one person's effort to find that which must always elude our grasp will be meaningful to others, and it's in that spirit of communal questing I offer this collection.

BOOK ONE:
Why We Do It

Arranged in order of composition, the poems in Book One encompass almost forty years. I was just 17 when I wrote "The Dance." I imagined my future, and now that that future has become my present, I look back at that lonely teenager and applaud the instinct that sent her out beyond the boundaries of conventional friendship to find companionship with all that is.

Maybe that's the theme of this portion of the collection, the initial 'why' we must swim a river of stone: to push past limitations to our growth. In "Dragon Dream," the persona wants to flee from emotional pain, but when she faces her fears, she discovers her soul. In "The Orphan" and "Black Magic," the persona needs to disentangle herself from oppressive relationships; in "New Day Dawning" and "Wealth," she struggles to free herself of crippling thoughts. "An Artist's Prayer" points beyond the confines of good and evil to an acceptance of life on its own terms; the eponymous poem of the collection, "Swimming the River of Stone," tackles those forces which impinge on collective fulfillment.

Several of the poems in this book rely on a chorus, a device borrowed from Greek drama. The chorus provides a running commentary on the persona's experience, and often duplicates her discovery process.

"An Artist's Prayer" was commissioned by the dancer and choreographer Janaki Patrik, who wanted to make accessible to a Western audience a portion of the Sanskrit verse epic, *Shiv Tandav Stotram*.

Swimming the River of Stone

Six of its stanzas were used here, wherein a king prays to the deity Shiva for the grace of *samsara*, perfect equanimity. He prays with such eloquence that his words become music, and Shiva, deeply moved by the king's art, grants him his request. The last six lines of the poem (beginning "O Beauty") are borrowed from the *Confessions* of St. Augustine of Hippo.

BOOK TWO:
Portraits from the Dreamtime

The three poems in Book Two arose from a collaboration. When I met the painter, Mary Frances Judge, at a party in 1988, we agreed that other artists – musicians, playwrights, dancers – often worked in partnerships that alleviated the loneliness of creative solitude and we wanted to try working together, so Mary Frances invited me to her studio to look at a new series of paintings she called "Transformations." She explained she'd asked people to donate articles of clothing and tell her the story surrounding the garment: the suit you wore to your first job interview, for instance, or the dress you had on when your husband proposed. The artist then worked clothing and paint together to honor those transitional moments in the subject's life, and the canvas became an abstract portrait of the storyteller.

That first day I went to the studio, the elevator opened and I was greeted by a swirling blaze of vibrant pinks and vivid oranges on a six-foot-wide canvas. I saw the vague outline of a frilly dress, and traces of glitter in the paint. "What do you think?" Mary Frances asked. "She looks all dolled up," I said, and the artist replied, "Well, her name is Dolly. What *else* do you think?" And our collaboration began.

I came to the studio daily, sitting in front of the paintings, gathering impressions, creating word-portraits of people I'd never met. I was studying shamanism at the time, focusing on the Australian Aboriginal concept of the Dreamtime. I understood this to be a spirit realm, a place beyond the confines of time and space. It seemed to me, sitting in front of canvases embedded with personal items and stories of life-changing events, that I could receive input about the subject from that beyond-place, much as a shaman might enter into the spirit realm to retrieve information that would empower the healing of a sick person.

Later, as I worked on the poems, I realized each of my subjects had become an archetype, because clearly insights about one person held true for many people. "Woman in a Man's World," for instance, began as a portrait of one woman who happened to be an art dealer in Chicago – Dolly had worn her frilly dress to an important opening – but I think the poem tells a story many women could claim as their own.

The creation of "First Female Astronaut" says something intriguing about the mysterious energies connecting us all. As I sat in front of Mary Frances' "Transformation" of her roommate, Wendy, I felt perplexed. I was picking up images related to war: blood, killing, nuclear holocaust. I hadn't actually met Wendy, but I had seen her going about her business on the periphery of the studio, and what I'd seen – a perky blonde college student who must have been a cheerleader in high school – just didn't jibe with the violent impressions I was receiving. I wanted to scratch out everything I'd written and go with my tangible, flesh-and-blood observations, but the images arriving at the tip of my pen were powerful and insistent, so I went with the less tangible but – as it turned out, more authentic – imaginative seeing.

After I finished the poem, Mary Frances told me that the clothing embedded in the painting was a jogging suit Wendy had worn on a trip to Europe, where she'd visited a World War II battleground in Belgium; where she'd been bloodied and almost killed by a bull in the famous Pamplona running of the bulls. I also learned from Wendy herself that underneath the mythic bear appearing in the poem was Wendy's childhood attachment object, a one-eyed stuffed teddy. And Wendy revealed, in a shocked whisper, that the "Mommy, I'm sorry" lines I thought my own were direct quotes from a play she had written a few years earlier.

Among the portrait poems, "The Gardener" stands out because I interviewed its subject, Olle Lindgren, a Swedish banker and economist. In fact, he commissioned this word portrait and its companion painting from Mary Frances and me. During the course of several conversations, Olle told me about his farm in the country, the one that had belonged to his grandfather. He told me about his hobby, restoring Mercedes cars with his son. He told me about his Morning Swimmers' Club; about his mentor; his rose garden; his cat, rescued from the boy next door, who was using her for target practice. And there were the things I could see for myself: his love for his own family, his protectiveness towards the human family, an unflagging enthusiasm for environmental concerns.

As my portrait-poem began to take shape from the interview material, I went to Mary Frances' studio to take impressions from her painting-in-progress. It was Martin Luther King's birthday. As I sat writing, I could hear noise from the loft below, which I knew to be a Chinese sweatshop, where immigrants worked long hours for little pay. Given Olle's background in economics, his passion for history and for the Earth, I thought these facts – the day's memorial and the sweatshop – needed to be included in the poem. During our interviews, Olle had struck me as a man at ease with his feminine, nurturing side and I wanted to weave that in as well.

BOOK THREE:
The Owl & The Stallion

Written in 1987, "The Owl & The Stallion" began as a love poem, and right from the start I thought of it as a fable, a fairy tale for adults. The animals are symbolic. They're the "redeemed" totem animals representing two of the nine points on the Enneagram, a system of spiritual growth through personality typing. The owl is point five in that system; the black stallion, point four. I won't say who's who, in terms of my love affair, but it doesn't really matter, because genders blur in this poem which transcends mere passionate attraction between a man and a woman. If called upon to articulate its theme, I would say "The Owl & The Stallion" is about the energies of transformation unleashed through the union of opposites. One could understand that union as a spousal bond between two people; as the integration of masculine and feminine principles within one individual; and, as the mystical marriage, the human soul's union with God.

A few notes are in order. First, the blood and water imagery in the poem is an allusion to Christ's crucifixion. (See John 19:34.) Second, the sparks that fall to earth to become "a new language no one/had heard before but everyone/understood it in whatever language they spoke" is an allusion to the story of Pentecost. (See Acts 2:1-11.) Third, the gaze between the owl and the stallion that initializes multiple transformations within the poem is a reference to the naked awareness that transpires between the soul and God in contemplative prayer.

BOOK FOUR:
Poems from the Noh

The poems in Book Four comprise a hitherto unpublished manuscript I completed in 1979. Included here is the original preface, which explains the artistic genesis of the work. I would like to note that all quotations from *The Classic Noh Theater of Japan* by Ezra Pound and Ernest Fenollosa (New Directions, 1979) are used in accordance with Fair Use Copyright law as it pertains to "new works 'remixed' from other material." And I'd like to take this opportunity to dedicate these poems to Bonnie Crown, my first literary agent, who has always loved them.

BOOK FIVE:
Songs from Silence

"Religion" is practically a four letter word these days. Many people have decided that dogma divides (it does); that religious practice is hypocrisy (it can be). Many people have packed up and moved away from organized, institutionalized belief systems. Most of us seem to be trying to carve out a God shaped space within using whatever tools come to hand, and I'm certainly in that camp now. There was a time in my life, however, when the dogmas and practices of the Roman Catholicism worked to bring me closer to the sacred mystery to which we give many names – that "virgin point" referred to earlier. During those years I didn't write very much (hence the "silence" in the title of Book Five), but when I did write, the poems emerged from a heady blend of passion and belief. I experienced an intense and heartfelt delight in the numinous, divine reality I glimpsed through and beyond the tenets of my faith tradition (hence the "songs" of the book's title).

These poems span six years, from 1980 to 1986. They include a linguistic approach to God-language I'd avoid were I writing today, but I've kept the language intact because it seems integral to the heart of that moment's experience. Now, for instance, I would not capitalize the pronouns "my" or "you" when referring to God or Christ, but I did then, so I've retained the usage. And since the poems rely heavily on the religious tradition that meant so much to me at the time, background explanations are necessary.

"Eucharist" is a meditation on Holy Communion as understood by Roman Catholics. It's written not from the receiver's but from Christ's point of view. Catholics believe that when a priest consecrates bread and ordinary wine during Mass, those items undergo a change of substance. They continue to look like bread and wine, but in reality they have become Jesus Christ, the fully human and completely divine God-Man. "Eucharist" references details about the passion and death of Jesus of Nazareth that appear in all four Gospel accounts. (See Mark 14 & 15; Matthew 26 & 27: Luke 22 & 23; John 18 & 19.)

"Baptism" was written as a kind of symphony, a tribute to the numinous possibilities heralded by the sacrament. It begins with a prelude: a statement about the reality of love. In the first movement, the persona meditates on her relationship to her Creator. In the second movement, the persona's reflections extend backwards in time and outwards to all of creation. She sees that the essential goodness of creation can be tainted by our negative choices. The third and final movement suggests that the life, death and resurrection of Christ is an antidote to the consequences of negative choices. The poem is, in effect, an attempt to write my way past the traditional doctrines of baptism and original sin into a more inclusive understanding. The last line of "Baptism" is an allusion to the poem "Sunday Morning" by Wallace Stevens, the bleak conclusion of which has us all flying "downward to darkness, on extended wings." Stevens shared the pessimistic outlook of most poets in the early and mid-20th Century, but faith had revealed to me an alternative possibility to which I wanted to give expression.

"Grave-Song" also arises from that time in my life when the articles of my faith were resonant with lyric significance. Christians profess belief in a triune God, which is traditionally defined as "three divine persons in one God." It's the second person of this Trinity – the Word of God – who became the man, Jesus of Nazareth. The day Jesus died horrifically on a cross is called *Good* Friday because Christians believe Jesus' death made life after death possible. Bad for Jesus, good for us. The birthing imagery in the poem is an allusion to this new life beyond the grave.

"Fire Flowers" is a retelling of the Gospel story of Pentecost as recounted in Acts 2:1-13. Briefly, forty days after Jesus' Resurrection, he "ascended into heaven," no longer walking among his companions in bodily form. Before his departure, Jesus had promised to send a "helper." His disciples didn't have a clue what that meant, but they trusted that this "Spirit of Truth" would show up, so they returned to Jerusalem to wait for it. When the Spirit arrived nine days later, it was accompanied by "a noise like a strong driving wind." And "there appeared to them tongues as of fire, which parted and came to rest on each one of them." After that, when the disciples preached in their native Aramaic their listeners could understand their words no matter what language they spoke. This miracle is referred to as the "gift of tongues," and I've alluded to it in another poem, "The Owl & The Stallion." I suppose it's every poet's dream, for her words to come alive in the hearts of her readers, and I'm fond of biblical passages which suggest this is God's dream as well.

"God Speaks from Within Your Heart" is another effort to get beyond the limitations of traditional God-language. Typically, the three persons of the Christian Trinity are referred to as the Father, the Son and the Holy Spirit. I wanted a gender-neutral language that would express the contemplative, non-dualistic spirituality to which I was drawn at the time of the poem's composition.

BOOK SIX:
Beckonings

Hurricane Gloria ripped through the northeastern United States in September 1985. I was a novice in a Ukrainian Catholic religious community then, and Gloria's visitation coincided with my monthly day of prayer. I'd already arranged to spend that day in a secluded hermitage we had on our property, and in the coming maelstrom, I sensed an invitation, a beckoning. It had something to do with prayer. With surrender. With trusting God to protect me from the storm.

Early in the morning of Friday, September 27, I went for a walk down by our lake. The wind was rising, but the rains held off. I sat on a stump by the shoreline and started to pray. When I looked at my watch, I was surprised to see that several hours had passed. The wind was stronger, the rain had started, and I ran back to my cabin to spend the rest of the day putting into words an experience beyond words.

Our community was, at the time, studying the rich musical heritage of our Byzantine rite. (The Catholic Church is larger than "Roman;" it includes Melkite, Ruthenian, Ukrainian and Maronite Catholics as well, who acknowledge the authority of the Roman pontiff but worship according to eastern, not western, traditions.) The community had been delving into *samohlasni*, a series of eight chant tones designated for the evening prayer service of Vespers, and the poems of Book Six asked for this solemn musical accompaniment even as they emerged from the tip of my pen, which is why I've included the musical notation for the poems.

As with poems in previous sections, Book Six contains numerous Biblical allusions, and some of the poems depend for their meaning on traditional Catholic Christian interpretations of doctrines such as the Incarnation, the Immaculate Conception (Mary's preservation from the effects of original sin), the virgin birth of Jesus, the Eucharist. I think readers familiar with these concepts will probably derive a satisfaction from the poems that could elude those unfamiliar with them, but I also believe the poems stand on their own as an expression of the unitive experience which is the summit of most spiritual traditions. I also believe such moments of wordless communion occur in everyone's life, regardless of their spirituality or the lack thereof. I would cite, as authority for the truth of this claim, the very last sentences of the Bible, alluded to in the third poem: "The Spirit and the bride say, "Come." And let everyone who is thirsty come. Let anyone who wishes take the water of life as a gift."

BOOK SEVEN:
Psalms for a New Millennium

In the Bible, the Book of Psalms is where the Hebrew people poured out their hearts to God in songs that are a moving testament to their yearning for intimacy with God in times of joy and sorrow, of praise and thanksgiving, of grief and anger. My book of psalms was written over a six-month period in 1993. I was living in New Mexico at the time, and had come to a crossroads in my relationship with God. I used the psalms as a model for working through my feelings which, as you can see, run the gamut from despair through anger into bliss. The Hebrew Psalter ends with Psalm 150. Mine begins with 151.

BOOK EIGHT:
Moments Out of Time

The poems in Book Eight gushed out – sometimes as many as three in the same day – over a one-month period in 2013. I had just finished, at age 62, the spiritual autobiography I'd begun when I was ten, which could account for that burst of creative energy. But what really stands out for me about these poems is how much *fun* they were to write. I've been writing poetry my entire life and while I have known many deep pleasures, I've never experienced anything approximating "fun," which the *Oxford English Dictionary* defines as "a diversion, amusement, sport; also, boisterous jocularity or gaiety."

BOOK NINE:
The Raven Chronicles

Ravens are ubiquitous in northern New Mexico, and when I moved there in 2000, I fell in love with them. Ravens are much larger than their crow cousins; their voices that much more hoarse, their bodies that much more dense. I decided to give Raven the last word in this book. If anyone knows how to swim a river of stone, it's Raven, who confesses to anyone who will listen, "I just couldn't be happy/ until I took you with me."

CONCLUSION
Why <u>Do</u> We Do It?

One day – I think it was in 1995, I think it was summer – I was walking around downtown Manhattan. I stopped to admire the world's first skyscraper, the elegant Flatiron Building, its modest 22 stories shaped like a 'V' to accommodate the triangular island lot formed by the convergence of Fifth Avenue, Broadway and 22nd Street. I looked up to the building's third floor, remembering I'd once participated in an arts conference there, just there, where the tip of the iron pokes into busy 23rd Street. I looked down to street level, and noticed a small, handwritten sign in a storefront window. "Sale on Scuba Lessons," it proclaimed, enticingly, and, since I'd been obsessed with underwater Nature shows for months, I said to myself, 'Why not?' and went in. I exited the store an hour later, lessons paid for, gear in a bag. It wasn't the discount that sold me, though, it was the look of yearning on the instructor's face when he said, in a reverent near-whisper, "It's so quiet down there, you can hear the shrimp cleaning themselves." He explained that "scuba" is an acronym for Self-Contained Underwater Breathing Apparatus, and the me that has always known how to breathe underwater sighed, relieved to discover it's only the apparatus that had been lacking.

I immediately set about writing a series of poems which was supposed to be about underwater adventure, but the eponymous poem of Book One – "Why We Do It" – was as far as I ever got. Just as New York's Flatiron Building marks the convergence of two major traffic arteries, the pearl image at the end of the poem merges two significant Gospel passages. The first is a parable told by Jesus. "The Kingdom of Heaven is like a treasure hidden in the field, which someone finds and hides again, joyfully selling everything to buy that field." The second is a comment Jesus made to a friend who was caught up in a harried moment of frustration and envy. "Martha, Martha," he said, "you are anxious and upset about many things, but one thing only is necessary."

This morning my crow friends walked on water. In New York City, the Flatiron Building stands sentinel over the point where two parallel lines intersect. Anything is possible, even breathing underwater, as long as we're willing to realign our priorities and commit ourselves wholeheartedly to the quest. Because, as spiritual teacher Richard Rohr explains, mystery is not unknowable, it is *infinitely* knowable. And this, I believe, is why we do it, whatever it is we're doing, why we search for it, whatever it is we're searching for: because infinity is within our grasp, if only our grasp be infinite.

BOOK ONE

THE DANCE

They tried to teach me to dance,
but I was as clumsy and unwilling
as a bear. My insides
were coiled all wrong
for a cha-cha. I wanted to move
in a circle.

I took for my models
the ballerina in my jewelry box,
a top, and the weather vane on our roof
when the wind blew hard.

I practiced at night.
First I learned how to support
my arms on air. Then,
that dizziness could be overcome
with a little effort. And finally
how the walls and furniture
translated into blur. That like foreign words,
smears of color had a familiar meaning,
and a slightly different sense.

I carried my discovery everywhere,
like a telescope, and focused my spinning
on all that I saw: trees, cows, houses.

My friends gave up. My whirling
had ruined me for serious dance.
I would never find romance,
they said.

And they were right. I have led
a solitary life, my only partners those
I could interpret for myself:
beasts suspended in air on their toes,
flowers dizzy, loose from their dirt,
and the sky, its farthest stars trailing
like a ballerina's skirt.

BLACK MAGIC
for Sam V

I

When you are away, I sleep
into your green embrace. In the rain forest
of my dreams, you grow wild
and carnivorous, swallowing me
into your strange stem.

When I wish to see you, I sleep
into your feathered caress. Plumes
a-bobbing, your precise beak
tears at my flesh.

When I am lonely for you, I sleep
onto the bed of herbs and branches you are
burning under me. You paint a red circle
on my chest, and bury your knife
in the middle of it.

II

We walk. We talk with human voices.
I can not see you clearly.
When you speak, your words accumulate
dark and heavy, but before they reach my ears
they turn to mist; like you, they are unpredictable.

Yesterday, I got you a book on gardening.
I know you have no interest in flowers,
but I do. I think
you and I are flowers. I think you and I

Why We Do It

are being uprooted by a blind gardener
with my face.

Lying beside you I see
a migratory path mapped into your eyes.
It is burned into your retina
and glimmers when you talk. Lover,
I have seen lights like that before,
in the eyes of winter-flying birds
resting in my yard. They left during the night
while I dreamt of shooting them, and now,
your breath comes evenly, and I am spitting
feathers from my mouth.
Your arm is bleeding.
Let me bandage it with this scarf.

III

When you approach me it is as if
you have been summoned by someone
who believes I am dying. I believe I am dying
but I didn't ask for you. Now
you've come with your dancing, with
your rattles and a mask carved like a bird's head.
You place it on my face and I breathe
through its beak a smell of green vines
and stale rain; through lidless eyes
I watch you pace a circle around my bed,
laying down leaves and feathers in
an ancient pattern. They are for healing,
you say. You say the spirits
inside me will be drawn out unresisting,
but it is I who rise:

> *This is a fire that I'm setting off.*
> *A splinter of stone which is white is the crane.*
> *And this is a fire that I'm lifting up.*

> A web of green on the sky is the palm.
> *The bird flies away.*
> We walk, we talk, we dance.
> *The branch shakes.*
> We walk, we talk, we dance.
> *This is a shadow that is burning.*
> *The arches of the sky break*

upon us.
I feel the rain
on my skin like silk.

IV

Last night, I dreamt I was removing
scarf after colored scarf
from between us. Each one
became its own story, and
told itself in its own language
until there was nothing left
of any of them except a low hum.

I woke, thinking of you, humming.

Dragon Dream

Pursued by dragons I have come to this place
to hide. Outside the world is wrapped in flames.
I can hear the forest, burning, the sky, burning,
the animals, crying as they burn.

CHORUS: This is the song of fire.
                Scorched wood,
                singed bone
                charred flesh,
                sang once
                and are silent.

I woke in the night and the dragons were there,
their whiskers lighting up my room. I ran,
and they ran behind me, and we left a path
of fire and ash.

CHORUS: This is the dance of fire.
                Scorched wood,
                singed bone,
                charred flesh,
                danced once
                and are still.

Now, they are sleeping, but their scaly eyelids
never close. They are wrapped in their wings
as if their wings were dreams.

CHORUS: We are singing the song
                    of the dragon's dream.
              We are dancing the dance
                    of the dragon's dream.

Book One

>We are singing and dancing
>for the dragon
>who cannot dance
>or sing
>or dream.
>
>He sits cold as rock
>in the midst of what he breathed to fire.
>>Our skin goes hot
>>and hotter
>>then ignites.
>
>But the dragon cannot shut his eyes.
>
>He sits hard as rock,
>his skin stretched on hollow bones.
>Everything melts around him.
>>Our bones
>>kindle
>>then melt.
>
>But the dragon cannot shut his eyes.
>
>His soul is a pearl
>he wears on his throat.
>>We blaze,
>>melt,
>>fuse,
>>we are
>>a pearl.
>
>But the dragon cannot shut his eyes.

There is no light inside this place.
The dragons have swallowed the sun and the moon.
I circle the room. I can see nothing,
but with my fingers I can feel carvings
on these four stone walls.

On the first wall is carved
a crab. I can tell
by its claws.

On the second wall is carved
a snake. It is coiled up,
but its mouth is closed.

On the next wall I can trace
a butterfly or moth. It has circles
etched on its wings.

And here, on the fourth wall,
is writing. I think
I have seen this alphabet before,
but I do not remember
when. This must explain
the carvings. How
will I ever learn
what they mean?

Here is the crab again.
And the snake.
And the moth.
And the writing.

And the crab and the snake
and the moth and the writing
The crab the snake the moth the writing ...

CHORUS: And we are turning,
          turning,
          faster, faster,
          around and around,
          from wall to wall ...

What is happening in me? I cannot withstand
this pressure! My bones are too big
for this sac of skin, my brain
too big for my skull.

    CHORUS: This is the song of the crab.
                     We are dancing the dance of the crab.
                     Inside our shell a shell has grown.
                     Under this rock we will wait
                        to split
                          out.

Who is this stranger who walks in my body?
I do not know
the face.
I want my own face
back again.

    CHORUS: This is the song of the snake.
                     We are dancing the dance of the snake.
                     Under our skin a new skin has formed.
                     The old one will peel
                     off.

What is happening to me?

    CHORUS: This is the song of the moth.
                     We are dancing the dance of the moth.
                     Now we will sleep,
                       but soon we will wake
                        to fly.

I must get out, out
from behind these walls
my eyes are walls it is
dark I crawl
from beneath one rock and find

Why We Do It

I am under another. I shed one skin,
and still a skin covers my bones. Tearing free
of one cocoon I am inside a cocoon ...

I remember

living.
I remember
I lived in the day and slept in the night.
I remember
I woke in the morning and slept in the night
but then I remember
I woke in the night and something inside me was hurting.
I screamed, but pain
came out, I ran,
but the pain ran with me, the pain was in me.
The world sang to the music but I couldn't sing.
The world danced to the music but I couldn't dance.
I couldn't sing I couldn't dance I couldn't dream I couldn't
die my God the pain!
This must be a dream!
It is wings.
I am flying.

I see the sun the sun is burning I swallow the sun.
I see the moon the moon is burning I swallow the moon.
I am burning ...

my skin
my bones
my life
burning ...

I am ...

O pressure!

Book One

O stranger!

My life!

I am

my God I am

        oh my soul!

    my soul

 *Why We Do It*

The Orphan

Last night I dreamt I was swimming in a white river.
The night before I dreamt I was in a dark forest filled
with red flowers ...

> CHORUS: She is making a catalogue
> of all her dreams. When
> she is finished she will have
> a grammar for the language of dreams ...

The night before that I dreamt I was being eaten
by birds, and the night before that I dreamt my tongue
was burning. Flames leapt from my mouth when I spoke ...

> CHORUS: Then she can begin
> translating her mother's novel.
> It is written in a language
> she does not understand.
> She can pronounce the words
> but does not know
> what the words mean.

Mehtor. Where is the dictionary large enough to explain
this word to me?

> CHORUS: At night, the hard bones
> of words dissolve
> into rivers of sounds
> she swims through
> to understand.

*mehtor meh tor meh breast breath neck protect caress meh
tor adore warm men tor protect adore caress adore
mehtor breast warm breath warm neck warm*

mehtor protect adore caress breast breath
mentor mother

* * *

"Dissolving into white rivers, bones flow through dark forests where magic flowers bloom."

    CHORUS: It is the first sentence.

I think this must be the scene, the place where the action will develop. But what will the action be?

    CHORUS: Whose bones
                        are dissolving?
                        What magic
                        do these flowers
                        perform?

Mother, when I speak to you my tongue burns.
Where does this fire come from? Burning
from an unknown source it is a strange flower grown
from strange, unknown seed.

    CHORUS: She scatters words
                        to the wind like seeds
                        which birds swarm around her
                        to devour.

How does this flower bloom? When I lie still I hear
my blood flow through my veins like wind through trees.

    CHORUS: There is no light
                        inside this forest.

I am on fire! I am filled with red blossoms of fire!
The heat melts my bones into rivers I can swim through ...

CHORUS: But what
            is she swimming
            towards?

                    *   *   *

Mother, this book of yours is a dream of you and I
am the dreamer. I am the language you invented. Trying
to find you in a translation of myself I find only myself.

CHORUS: And who knows what
            she means?

I longed for you, and my longing turned to birds.
They flew back into the past trying to find something of you,
anything at all, your breast, your warm breath, your caress,
but they found nothing, and returned to me.

CHORUS: And now the birds
            are hungry,
            and real.

Where is the book large enough to explain any of this to me?

Last night I dreamt I was swimming in a river that flowed
through a forest. On the river's banks red flowers bloomed
in thick profusion. Birds whirled around me, diving at me,
and when I tried to scream flames leapt from my mouth ...

CHORUS: From generation to generation,
            deep in the bone,
            desire
            is fire
            and it burns.

Thoughts for a New Decade
(New Year's Day, 1990)

One.
Stay true to yourself. Keep close
to your own center, like
the flame wrapped 'round
a candle's wick.

Two.
Find
some like-minded souls.
You will know them the same way swans
recognize each other, calling
forever
across their lake of stars.

Three.
Remember that a small, delicate voice
of great
purity carries
further, floats
higher and touches
more hearts than a strong
loud sound. This revelation
is old-hat stuff
to angels.

Four.
When the bad days come, hang on. Picture
a swan rising up on great
wings rising up
into the sky becoming
an angel becoming

Why We Do It

a new constellation: stars
taking the form of
an angel carrying a candle in its right hand. Then whisper
to yourself, "That's me
up there."

AN ARTIST'S PRAYER

In Memorium, Lucille Cummings

Drumroll,
birdwing, wavesand, tiretread, rainpour, footmarch,
hammerpound: beat and sound make
music: notes like parrots
flapping through trees, like goldfish
flashing in ponds. Rainbows ashimmer, spiderwebs
aquiver: motion and rest make
the dance: in
and out, pulse
in, pulse
out: heart,
lungs,
gills, breath
in, breath
out, aflicker in the vein the dance is: light
and shadow, good
and bad, high
and low, quick
and slow: iron and flint struck to spark: life
and light and love make fire.
The living light grows bright like fire.
The loving life consumes like fire:
broad green leaves and fat green stem:
gnarled stub charred by lightening streak.
Sweet birdsong, silver chapel bells:
the cawing crow, the funeral dirge.
Turn and turn and turn around:
crescent moon to noonday sun.
Turn and turn and turn around:
black sky, studded with stars,

blue sky, scudded with clouds.
Turn and turn and turn and the ground shakes, earth
quakes: music
of the spheres: comets
crashing, supernovas
exploding, black holes
imploding: dance
of the years: dinosaurs lumber, glaciers rumble,
turn and turn and turn me around, let me dance!
With the soft breeze on my right and the hurricane
on my left. Gentle rain above, flood stream
below: allowing it all, smiling at it all, entranced,
delighted, amazed by it all. Not pushed,
not pulled, not caught, not trapped, not fooled,
not tricked, free
I shall dance: across the edge
of the sword, the head
of the pin, on the crest of the wave, in the eye
of the storm, let me laugh! Laughter
in the song of the bird. Laughter
in the beat of the drum. In the rustle of the leaves, the trill
of the flute: flutesong, windsong, drumsong, birdsong,
my song, let me sing!
Sing with pleasure in the dreariest things:
spackling a wall, washing a dish. Sing
the perfection of overlooked things:
one black fly, an uncooked egg.
Sing sorrow, sing joy, sing pain and peace, I'm alive!
Living, let me love, loving,
let me be light, O Beauty, so ancient
and so new,
> keep me deep in,
> hold me close to,
> forever and always, only
> what is true.

CIRCUS FAMILY

The circus
is in town the paper says the Guerreros
are the only troupe in the world performing the Seven
Man Pyramid without safety rigs. Four men
walk the high wire balancing two
aerialists who balance
a third but they're worried
they can't do it
with the chair on top an accident
last month paralyzed Wolfer
from the waist down family
pitched in to save the act because it's better
that way no matter how tired
or troubled each thinks
of the other: it's my sister, my wife,
my sister's husband strangers
can't be trusted. A recent replacement almost killed them all,
going for the platform to save himself.

Gape-mouthed, I read how Arturo, the father,
never used nets, said they detract from the excitement
of the act how Ruth, the mother,
walked the wire tightly girdled
through eight pregnancies how the children
balanced on low ropes from the time
they could walk how Jenny and Werner,
sleeping, had to be wedged
against the wall or nightmares of falling
would make them cry out how Jahaida
ran away with the elephant trainer. Four months later
she was back now Brian
has left his elephants to join her

in the act, just as Aura
left her earthbound people (clowns for seven generations)
to be with Werner up on the wire.

I think of flat, wide places: the desert.
The ocean. Think
how the horizon stretches between earth and sky like a taut wire.
Next morning
I'm in a long line, buying
a ticket for the circus. I buy it
for the same reason I go to church: I need
to be there. I need
to watch someone act out
my beliefs and desires although,
waiting in line, I cannot name
my beliefs and desires. I carry
my ticket for two days, a pledge, a promise. Of what,
I wonder, as the houselights
dim. While monkeys cavort in Ring Two,
in a darkened Center Ring they rig the tightrope.
When the spotlight shifts the Guerreros are up
in the air I gape at the relentless floor
and when they pray, *En el nombre de Dios,*
I pray with them for I, too,
have been carried on a tightrope from the womb, practicing
my balance since earliest childhood, trained
to risk, plagued
by nightmares of falling so it must be for me
they inch their way across a high, thin wire, seven
people stitched together like a crazy quilt
when Christ was asked,
How often must I forgive he answered,
Seven times seven times now the Seven
stop for Aura to rise from her chair her legs
tremble, every muscle straining to whisper If I slip
we all fall and in the darkened stadium seven thousand
strangers are stitched together like a crazy quilt because

in the same paper I read about the circus I also read
that a woman who was blinded by her jealous lover
married him when he got out of jail that a tourist
had his hand chopped off because
he didn't surrender his wallet
fast enough that a death sentence
was commuted to life because four jurors say
they convicted the man on a gut feeling
he was guilty and there are new bombings
in Ireland and Israel and 50,000 children
will starve to death today we are all inching
across the same
high wire if one slips
we all fall no one
gets to the platform alone.

Why We Do It

THE SEVENTH WAVE

I

At Long Island's easternmost tip, gulls twirl
above the waves like ribbons unfurled from spools.
Their plaintive cries remind me:
whoever would belong to earth and sea and sky at once
might never find a home.

Two years since I was here.
The ocean rushes to greet me with open arms,
an old friend whose face has changed:
sandbars where there had been none,
a tier of dunes where there had been level beach,
and I, too, have changed: face
more lined, flesh
more slack, hair
all gray now, yet
I can hoof it two miles into town,
hoist groceries onto my back and return,
still lively enough to note
that each round pebble at the sea's edge
makes twin dimpled tracks in the sand,
as if the ocean thought it might lose its way,
left these marks to find itself again.

Yes. And the wind has rippled the beach like a fish's fin,
and the sand is littered with the footprints
of forgotten gulls and dogs,
and the golden light of the afternoon
sun pools in my footprints,
then the water fills them, then they're gone.

Yes. Waverack clings to the sea, and pinerack
clings to the hills. I bend down,
scoop up a piece of driftwood, surface smooth as a mirror.
I see emerald leaves, thick trunk, stout limbs, roots
that cling, all melted down to this sliver of woodrack I hold
in one hand. And the sand that peppers my memento?
A mountain, this speck? A shell, this glint? They say
all life on earth began in the sea, so, at the sea's edge
life melts back to its end. Alpha and Omega. First and last.
The dead gull I stumbled on, going in,
a ribbon wound back on its spool:
once-bright eyes clogged with sand, beak closed forever, yet
its wings were splayed out in a graceful S: that corpse
was poised for flight.

Yes. And I am for home now, to feed this would-be corpse.
Before I turn away, I watch the waves, how the water
heaves itself crestward, breaks, collapses
onto shore. I try to count them, wondering
is it true, what I read, that they come in sets of three
marked out by a single wave, the seventh, the highest?
But I think you must stand still
as a mountain, have eyes sharp as a gull's,
before you can find such a pattern and my eyes
have found something else, far out, near the horizon:
a pod of seals at play out there, where
earth and sea and sky meet, yes, and I lumber up
through the dunes, awkward
as a beached seal, arms akimbo, poised for flight, looking for home.

II

The sea plagues pebbles to sand, and the desert
worries rocks to dust.
This beach is brown, and I await sunset perched
on a gray log, remembering
that other realm of gray and brown. Once,

Why We Do It

up on a mesa, I found
a black spume of volcanic rock. Like a wave
heaving itself crestward it curled, and perched
on that ancient billow I looked
up. Low clouds
dot a blue sky like whitecaps and above
that ruffled surface, hawks
ride thermals like gulls. I am a diver, gliding
between cratered hills. Cactus
jut out, sharp as coral, and the green tentacles
of the palo verde tree riffle in the wind's current while wings
of passing birds ripple the air like fish fins I cannot
stay here long I look
up to that shimmering curtain behind
that shining veil beyond which
I belong the sky
bursts into flame and when day's ashes settle I still perch
on a black log on a black beach by a black ocean looking up
into a black sky.

Yes. And that smear of light is a comet,
last seen four thousand years ago when the Great Pyramids
were new and the great empires
of Greece and Rome were yet to come, civilizations
heaving themselves crestward, collapsing
onto some shore, yes,
and the milk white froth of the breakers
and the milk white froth of the comet's tail
and some one wave is the seventh, the highest, marking out
a pattern. In diving school they showed us
how every seven feet another color
disappears from the spectrum. Yellow,
gone, orange,
wiped out, red,
vanished until only blue
remains, blue
sea, blue

sky, Alpha, Omega, first,
last all of us
on earth winding back
on our spools, furled
up, finally
home.

Why We Do It

NEW DAY DAWNING

It must have been the moon.
In night's black field, a pearl-white seed ...
on my sleeping body,
an opalescent sheen ... at dawn, I wake, thinking,
'Surely I'm at least as good as this.' This
rising sun that warms my walk through woods, to
River's edge ... this yellow wisp of flower hidden
near the path ... surely I'm at least as lovely.
At least as sweet as this tiny chit of chickadee.
Important, like this bee. Of value, like the pollen
he carries, invisible, on his wings.
And this water, broken
in its fall over sharp rocks – don't I cry too?
And laugh after, like this trilling stream?
This dragonfly, this airborne sapphire stick – am I
less well made? These herons,
their avid seeking, their
scrabbled cries – are my needs less real?
Where River's fingers claw the earth, tear dirt
away by fistsful, an old oak bends low, naked roots
exposed. From water's depths some green heaving
drapes oak's crippled legs like a skirt.
Turning away, I wonder, How long
will these roots hold? Some deep heaving drapes the naked question:
As long as I can, I sigh.

Here, soft mud holds the stamp of River's rippled surface,
and one sunbeam fixes two objects in lucent shimmer.
The pearly gleam: a broken oyster shell.
The diamond sparkle: a shard of soda bottle.
Each worn smooth by wind and water, each lying
in a graceful arc ... so hard to tell.

Made by divine? Made by human hands?
A hundred years ago, a factory stood on this spot.
Busy men harvested ice from the frozen Hudson,
shipped it down to New York Harbor where, today,
8 millions mouths open in an avid, scrabbled cry.
Worn to stumps, this old pier's pilings hump
among moss-clung rocks
like decayed teeth in earth's open mouth,
and every tiny leaf floating on River's surface
casts a tiny swimming shadow on the silt below.
A cloud passes overhead, its shadow
on gold green leaves a tremolo. Everything
is possessed of an alien element. Water
carries earth, earth carries sky,
nature carries us, and over it all, the shadow
of something sacred passes.

My great-great grandfather fought in the Civil War,
and his great grandfather fought in the Revolution. Commerce and war sometimes seem
our greatest achievement, yet
somewhere in the dark and troubled field called life,
a bright seed grows.
No matter what hard questions heave from what
unknown depths, we can
hold on. And one fine day we will wake, knowing
we are good, like God's own moon.

WEALTH

Today I have trekked uptown to Christie's Art Emporium,
to see the Ganz collection before it's sold
for more millions than I have fingers and toes.
Between downstairs lobby and upstairs gallery,
a large Matisse greets me. In 1953,
when I was three years old, Matisse and I
were making paper cutouts, but his wild spirals,
outlined in thick black like finger paint,
carry a price tag of six million dollars.

The rooms are crowded, and I wonder if my shoulders
might be rubbing against the shoulders of someone
considering a purchase. Where do you put
a six million dollar painting?
How many times a day should you look at it?
I'm glad I don't have to decide. Instead,
I want to stick Redon's flowers in my mouth,
because they look like fruit. I'd like that yellow juice
dribbling down my chin. In a second Redon,
St. George seems already to have slain his dragon.
It sinks into the leftmost corner of the sea, dissolving,
like sunset, into a blaze of red and purple.
One of these works is more expensive,
and I can't helping asking myself, Why?
In the Middle Ages, because some paints cost more
than others, patrons would specify, this
percentage of gold, that
of cobalt blue, thereby proving their status
for all the world to see. Which painting would Redon prefer?
Is that him I hear crying, true mother at Solomon's knee?

Braque's "Country Estate." The trees
are bright pink and the grass, a vivid blue.
In Kindergarten, I painted a carrot tree.
When Miss Simon held it up for the class to laugh at
she hissed, "Everyone knows carrots don't grow on trees."
I wish Miss Simon were here. Crazed vegetation
is going for four million.

Renoir, Cezanne, Monet, Van Gogh, I'm getting dizzy
from beauty, and these zeros
are melting into thick black spirals. 'Thank God
I can't afford to buy one,' I whisper, then remember,
not many days ago, I stood at the sea's edge,
with a wild wind spiraling sand into my mouth and eyes, as if
it would fill my empty spaces. Onto the beach,
a crazed ocean had flung shells, each more perfect
than the next. Greedy, I snatched
at every one I saw, disappointed: all
were broken by the sea's churning. Only
because sand filled them were they whole, only
because they lay where the sea left them. And who am I
to sit in arrogant judgment on the wealthy,
when there is so much I cling to
as if it were my own?

SWIMMING THE RIVER OF STONE

I

This I have learned from the desert:
to know a thing, you must become that thing,
dip yourself in it like pen in ink,
let it write you in its own words.

A river once flowed through this land.
On the first day of the new year I chanced upon it,
> soft curves scooped into hard rock
> by the press of water, bottom
> crushed to gravel by the wild hammering of water,
> a deep gash carved by water's chisel,
> a flowing line sculpted by water's hand.

Dawn tugged me from sleep today.
Like the hurt in a phantom limb,
the ancient trilling of the River of Stone wells up in my heart:
an old story wants to tell itself new, a secret
asks to be shared. Find the Source, the River said.
Not enough to stumble on some turn or jag.
Today you must come as pilgrim.
Today you must bring them all.
Past and present and future generations,
black and white and red and yellow generations,
native and immigrant, old and new, born and not born,
all of them stretched out like a mighty "V," geese
migrating home. Find the Source, the River said.

And when the stars paled to naught but memory,
and with the last quarter moon still bright in the sky,
I saw craggy mountains take their places for a dance,

I heard flat-topped mesas clap rhythm with their hands.
I set out across the trackless desert, not bothering
to plan the way for in this place of everything the same
and nothing different, everything different
and nothing the same, the easy way
will turn hard, the hard way,
easy, the path shows itself only
in the going, in the putting
one foot in front of another. I put
one foot in front of another, walking, walking.
Every few steps a new landscape, every landscape
a new history:
> in this ravine, a forest of *palo verde*,
> in this gully, red red rock.
> Here, the earth's crust is razor sharp, like lava.
> Here, the ground is smooth, like concrete.

Walking, walking:
> this is the hill of sage, purple in spring.
> This is the hill of yellow grass.

I name these places as I name the parts of myself,
as we name the parts of ourselves:
> these are the people who came from the east, hungry.
> These are the people who came from Africa, forced.
> These are the people
> who were already here, displaced.

Find the Source, the River said.
In the trackless desert of the centuries which have gathered us all together, an ancient trilling wells up in our hearts.
Walking, walking. Putting one foot in front of another.
The path is in the going.

II

A hunting hawk cries overhead.
I am now where the River began.
Let me live, she rasps. Tell them all I want to live.
Walking, walking.

Why We Do It

Deep inside this wound of River.
Gone the desert with its wide open vistas.
Gone the familiar landmarks: mountain, mesa, nearby town.
Here, now, only River is real:
glistening rocks remember water,
hard packed banks wait for water,
pebbled bottom mistakes footsteps for water, and
this tree doesn't even know the water's gone.
Still stands green on its island where River
once split around it. I touch
its shredding bark, arthritic trunk, begging
a blessing for us all:
let us be unmoved by the superficial.
Let our roots plunge strong and deep,
seeking always the one necessary thing.

Walking, walking.
Arms and legs churning like water.
Death is everywhere.
Bleached white by sun, sanded smooth by dust and wind,
inch by inch the dry bones of cactus grow back to nothing.
Walking, walking.
Life is everywhere.
Sprouts from split rock, clings
to stones, flits
by, pale and yellow.
Here, a six-armed giant, already alive
when America was born.
Can you show us how it's done?
Riddled with holes where the cactus wren nests,
you turn flute when the wind blows.
Sing. Of sun and dust and wind.
Of the bleached bone you will become when you topple.
From our dying, what can save us?
From our living, who will fashion a song?

Book One

Walking, walking.
A sharp "S" and, at its tail, a rippled spill of gray rock.
Down. Down.
Six. Eight. Maybe ten feet. Hands
claw boulders, face
presses stone, body
stretches, unfolds, down, down, like the fall
of water, let
go, drop, like a splash of water
onto rock.
I hunker down in River's adamantine womb.
Listen for her petrified heartbeat, feel for her pulse,
locked in stone. Mother of us all, we are locked in stone.
We feared thirst when the River was flowing and now
the River is gone. We stumble on through meaningless days,
purposeless nights, craving
we know not what. Crippled by flagrant abuses.
Lamed by secret crimes.
Small infidelities mound to huge betrayals: we cannot see.
Whispered yearnings crescendo
to loud moaning: we cannot hear.
To whom shall we turn for new eyes, new ears?
Who can make us walk again, proud and free and strong?
How can we implore divine assistance, when our language
is tainted, our very alphabet, profaned, yet

every heart holds an ancient impress.
Remembers water.
Waits for water.
And deep within the wound
which once was water's living course
some green and secret tree still stands,
strong roots plunged deep to the Source.
No need for pilgrim journeys.
No need to search for home.
This desert moment is flowing, can you see?
This flowing is a mighty torrent, can you hear?

Why We Do It

We are the River.
Past and present and future generations,
black and white and red and yellow generations,
native and immigrant, old and new, born and not born,
cascading down the centuries,
spilling out across today,
surging toward tomorrow.
We are the River.
We are writing a new story, in words
which cannot be hidden.
Freedom, yes. Equality, yes. Abundance, yes.
For all. Yes. We are the River.
We can make the parched land exult.
We can make green what once was waste.
We are the River. Ours is the power. And the glory.
We are the River. This we know.
We know.
We know.
We are the River.
This we know.

WHY WE DO IT

Last night I dreamt I was dreaming
of a barren, cratered landscape pocked with ancient stones.
Burned by sun and swept by wind, the soil
had turned to sand. Giant cactus loomed,
misshapen arms thrust up to the sky,
begging for rain. Thirsty, I walked alone,
neither pursued nor pursuing, neither sought nor seeking,
while above me, stars wheeled in vast constellations,
and the moon gleamed like a huge tear, frozen.

When I woke I was a diver, suspended
in some nameless ocean,
tank of compressed air strapped to my back.
In this silent realm I swam, the stranger, the alien,
the explorer, searching
for something, some sunken treasure, some priceless pearl,
while all around me,
in colored constellations, schools of fish whirled.

When I woke at last, the moon shone through my window
like a pearl, and the barren shadows of leafless trees
were etched on my wall like coral.
Weeping, I thrust needy arms to the sky
in wordless supplication

and knew then what I know now:

that each moment is an ocean,
and in each moment we hang suspended,
while improbable creatures of impossible beauty wheel around us.

Why We Do It

That compressed to the finite the Infinite
is a thirst: a naked bare seeking, the unknowable
made known as much in what it reaches for
as in what it is afraid to reach.
That what holds us together
is the same as what keeps us apart.
And that we are all divers.
Strangers, aliens, explorers.
Swimming in our silent moment.
Searching for our pearl.

Book Two

Portraits from the Dreamtime

WOMAN IN A MAN'S WORLD

Hinged
    on dawn and sunset day's door swings
        open with a pink
            creak and Dolly swings out
                into the world. Dressed
            to kill she
                tip taps daintily
down the street flouncing
    among the flannel suits like a hibiscus
        among cabbages. With appointments
            lined up like pegs
                in a pinball machine
                    Dolly careens
                into
her accountant's office. Bells
    clang, lights
        flash, score
            tallies, she slides
                some papers across
                    the desk, saying,
                "I know
that's the rule, dear, but don't you think
    life's something more than
        a traffic light?" Dolly laughs
            like yeast. In the bowl of his face,
                the man's smile rises
                but the woman
                    is up and gone,
off to tour a General Motors plant. When
    she passes, three conveyor belts
        stop dead in their tracks. As
            baffled foremen yell and VPs

                              shuffle nervously
                                    on Wingtipped feet
Dolly giggles and points. "He looks
     like a tulip," the woman
             cries and the men
                   bray like donkeys because
                        the mechanic's upturned
                              red-uniformed
rear end bobs
     back and forth on the stalk
          of his legs but Dolly's
                on her way again. Board rooms,
                      executive suites, she whips
                            through them all
like a cone-shaped wind leaving papers, plans, projects
     to dance behind her like dervishes.
          From the hushed
                lunchtime gabble Dolly's voice rises
                      like a helium balloon, floats
                            to the ceiling
and hangs there. Businessmen
     finish their third
           martini while Dolly signs the check
                 with a pink pen, tweaking
                      the maitre d's cheeks
                            on her way out
the door and now it's a conference room
     where late afternoon sunlight filters
           through Venetian blinds. Phrases
                float like dust motes: "elected
                      not to renew ... notice
                            of termination ... cured
in a subsequent period ..." as the words
     swirl around her head Dolly watches
           the shadows of pencils scribbling
                 across yellow legal pads. "They look
                       like logs," she thinks, and

                imagines them
stacked in some clearing way out
   in the forest. "Who
      will live there," she wonders then feels herself
         bend down over a wood
            stove taking out hot biscuits
               for supper baby
stirs in sleep the woman
   tips the cradle into a rocking
      motion then the door
         swings open ... "Could you repeat
            your question?" Dolly asks
               the lawyer but
the answer
   is lost as the door
      bangs closed her husband
         is home he sways
            like a tulip on the stalk
               of his legs his smile
rises the woman
   laughs, tweaks
      his cheeks runs her hands
         across his flannel
            shirt night
               is coming
then .... "Let's call it a day," the lawyer
   announces. Dolly
      sighs. Walks
         home. Watches
            sunset. Yearns
               for a door to swing
open, bang closed.

FIRST FEMALE ASTRONAUT

                     Earth
solid, earth
   dense, earth full, earth
      round, earth masses
         out presses
           in dips
              down mounds
                 up soft
rain falls silent
   mist rises hiss
      of breeze sways
         sweet scent of wheat of grass of green
            growing over massed
               mountains over dipped
                  valleys sends
crisp colors into leaves, fruit
   bulges then
      heavy snow hushed
         on mountaintop, valley
            deep then buds
               swell forth breast
                  of earth heaves
soft hiss of breeze sways
   sweet scent of green
      growing.

                   Wendy
walks forth on girdled
   asphalt streets on fist
      of concrete closed
         tight, under needling
            skyscrapers past ripping

Book Two

>   jackhammers whizzing
>   cars Wendy walks with solid
>   feet heavy-shod, soft
>   curves shrouded, smile
>   flung out like a protective arm
>   fending off
>   faceless passersby
> who trod and plod, Wendy
>   rushes through lecture halls where science
>   probes history
>   dissects philosophy
>   rips questions
>   bulldoze her heart,
> answers leave it strip-mined Wendy whizzes
>   to airport
>   hustle-bustle
>   through airport
>   hurley-burley high
>   above the Atlantic,
> Wendy watches from behind thick paned windows
>   as waves plead like upturned faces, straining
>   for shore like babies
>   for the breast, sadness
>   swells Wendy's heart, flows
>   forth to mix with
> jet plane exhaust streaming out over
>   sea's hungry mouth until,
>   exhausted, she leans
>   her head against the glass,
>   whispers, "This
>   is too much I can't
> take this anymore," falls
>   into troubled sleep.
>   Wendy dreams of a great she-bear curled
>   in her cave while snow hushes
>   mountaintop, valley
>   deep inside her brain

Portraits from the Dreamtime

```
fingers of memory close
    like a fist: last season's
        litter the season
            before that the season
                before that, faceless cubs
                    probe her fur
with needling
    claws tug
        her dugs with hungry
            mouths then waking, she
                rises, shakes
                    shaggy fur, lumbers
out to sniff first scent of green
    growing but earth
        is gone all
            is black like a cave's
                vaulted roof, paws
                    turn into gloved
hands and booted
    feet, snout
        turns into helmet, fur
            crinkles into a metallic
                suit, the lone astronaut
drifts through space, lifeline
    dangling like a severed
        umbilical cord, inside her brain a fist
            opens from behind
                thick paned visor she whispers,
```

```
                        "I remember
heat like an icy shroud
                        I remember
highways snapping like garters
                        I remember
skyscrapers buckling like crumpled clothes
```

                              I remember
flesh flashing into photo
negatives, skeletons akimbo like crazed
X-Rays, shadows seared
into sidewalks
                              I remember
tidal waves and quakes, earth's
womb giving one final cramped
heave then fire like blood
gushing then
ash falling a hush
like snow then a merciless
sun a violent
wind a swirl
of sand whirl
of continents into one
vast desert then dust
trailing into the sky."

                              Wendy
whimpers in sleep, pressed
    into airplane seat she curls
        her arms around herself feels
            flesh dense and
                solid, full and
                    round, still
dreaming she whispers,
    "Mommy, I'm sorry, Mommy,
        I won't do it again, Mommy
            forgive me, Mommy,
                love me again." Tears fall
                    soft as rain, she wakes,
rises: plane has dipped down on runway, passengers
    smile, mound
        out through open
            door sending crisp
                footsteps down hallways,

            sidewalks into whizzing
cars, Wendy's smile swells, buds, breast
    heaving she breathes
        deeply, sighs
            a sweet scent of green
                growing, walks forth onto

        Earth.

THE GARDENER

I

If there were light,
in winter,
in Sweden.

If there were light,
on the man's face,
in the car,
on the road
outside Stockholm.

If there were light (but there is no light),
it would just
be breaking now, just
fingering the east as if straightening
night's bedclothes and the light
would reveal a smile just
breaking on the man's face, as car and driver press
into the silky wet forest, bush
of fir trees stiff
along the road, swaying
in the wind, moaning as the man drives deeper
and deeper into the dark woods, face lit up
to remember Birgitta
as he left her this morning, covers
bunched up under her, like a little girl
she'd looked, and straightening them over her, yes,
oh, yes, like I used to do for Karl Johan, the son
so like the mother, it's Ylva
who sleeps like me, ramrod
straight as if guarding

Portraits from the Dreamtime

her dreams, oh, Birgitta this morning, lying
defenseless like a sleeping child, oh, pity, for the things
that can't take care of themselves, the man's heart swells
in his chest, oh, sorrow
like sap, oh, joy like green growing, his heart
stiffens, pushing deeper
into the pliant darkness, ninety, a hundred, a hundred and ten
kilometers, plunging on, pulse
racing, pounding in rhythm with the tires on the road, why
these strings, I would fly free but these strings
'round my heart, like a kite held down, my heart,
yesterday evening, out back of the house,
me with my '66, Karl Johan with his '63, those old Mercedes,
now they look like new, walking over to Karl Johan
with those sparkplugs in my open hand but oh,
my tall blonde son, matched
bookend to oh, my tall blonde daughter, face
smeared with grease, oh, these two will inherit the earth?
Will be deep in earth's toil, steeped
in earth's care, oh, mercy
on these creatures so fragile, so frail, the man's heart bulges
in his chest, turgid with tears he will not shed, sparkplugs
forgotten in his still-open hand, he'd blurted it out,
the same question Axel Oxenstierna
had asked his Karl Johan some three hundred years ago,
"Don't you know, my son, with how little wisdom
the world is governed?" Yes,
oh, yes, the man sighs, hands tighter on the wheel,
they are *grön jord*, green earth, I surround them like *blå himmel*, blue
sky, it holds,
enfolds, envelops, protects, life
is like *träd*, rooted
in earth the tree reaches up
to the sky, rain
comes, after
the rain, all things grow, after the rain
that's the best time for mushrooms we set out then,
in summer, on grandfather's farm, mine now, Birgitta and I,

trailing behind our two grown children who swing baskets
they once slept in, such peace, in the forest, the fat
caps of mushrooms swell
over their straight, stiff stalks, peace
in the wet, moist earth, peace
in the musky smell of earth,
baby, barn, *tonåring*, man, *kvinna*,
baby, child, adolescent, man, woman, eyes shining
with unshed tears, the man glances at his watch.
Soon, he thinks, the old general, he'll be waiting
on his front porch, he'll
give his ritual salute, jump in, we'll be off
to *Morgonbadarklubben*, Morning Swimmers' Club:
water polo, sauna, late lunch, home by two what
to do with a Saturday afternoon in the land
of perpetual darkness, the kitchen
floor? Paint the spare room? Fix
that window near the garden, oh, the *trädgård*.

The man smiles.

My garden.

For there will be light.

It is dark now but when winter is over.
(For it will be over.)

When spring comes.
(For it will come.)

When the ice melts.

When the *snö* disappears and ice becomes *vatten*.

When the *fågel* begins to *vissla* in the *träd*, yes,
oh, yes, the man sighs, I'll prune, I'll snip, I'll tend
my roses, Hickotea, she will soak up the sun from the hot

flagstones, her old bones glad for the comforting warmth,
her gray brown fur blends in with the gray brown
stones, I have to be so careful
where I step, old Aunt Moster, that first time I saw her,
scrawny little creature fleeing her role in the drama next door.
Boisterous and belligerent, the neighbor's child intent
on being a great world leader, pretending
he's Cyrus II, Alexander the Great, Gengis Khan, Hannibal,
Napoleon, Patton. Tiny little kitten, sick of make-believe,
tired of playing mercenary from Thessaly,
bowman from Crete,
Viking sailor,
American marine, helpless little, sweet little thing, worn out
from being lunged at with spears, shot at
with arrows, pierced with darts, ripped apart
by shrapnel, bombed with Napalm, weary
of daily re-enacting Marathon, Hastings,
Waterloo, Gettysburg, Iwo Jima ...
laughing out loud at the boy's puffed-up chest,
his knockneed swagger, his
King-of-the-Mountain, Top-of-the-Heap-strut,
yes, oh, yes, the man sighs, laughing again.
His tires crunch on the gravel drive and the old general salutes.

II

Rational
and resolute, Mr. Karl Olof Lindgren, Senior
Vice President and Chief
Economist of Skandinaviska Enskilda Banken, approaches
the speaker's platform to address the quarterly meeting
of the National Business Economic Issues Council
on the subject of the free capital movement
in Nordic countries impacting on venture capital
for environmentally benign infrastructure investments.

(*Hans rosor är rotade i hans fotsulor.*)

Book Two

Rational
and resolute, Mr. Lindgren glances
around the conference table as he steps
to the podium, yes, oh, yes, they're all here,
members of the National Advisory Council
for Environmental Technology Transfer,
Business Development Managers
for Chase Manhattan Bank, N.A., Banco Atlantico, S.A.,
Barclays Bank, PLC, numerous corporate vendors,
a few investors and representatives
from the academic community here to observe.

(*Hans rosor är rotade i hans fotsulor.*)

Rational
and resolute, Mr. Lindgren begins
by quoting Gahlin's definition
of an economist as a person who,
with hindsight, is able to tell people how much
they would have lost if they had followed
his advice but behind
the words spoken are words
remembered, how Erik
would smile and say, "All
we have to do, Olle, is persuade the world's statesmen
and the governing bodies of the central banks
to take a somewhat more sensible view of things."

(*Hans rosor är rotade i hans fotsulor.*)

Rational
and resolute, Mr. Lindgren develops his theme of price
determination, balanced growth and capital formation.
Erik always said vested
interests are dangerous
illusions and we should use the family tradition
as a model for solidarity but how,
he wonders, as he asks

that the lights be dimmed.
Mr. Lindgren has slides: infrared maps, laser photos
taken by satellite, earth revealed
as a round globe aswirl with light and shadow,
perpetual movement caught in a still moment, it looks like
leksaks boll, a giant toy ball, yes, oh, yes,
and glancing again around the table he thinks,
a ball tossed about by boisterous, belligerent children.

(*Hans rosor är rotade i hans fotsulor.*)

Rational
and resolute, in a cool, steady voice, Mr. Lindgren explains
which winds blow acid rain over the fir forests
of Sweden, the timber regions
of Russia, the redwood preserves
of the American Northwest, "We must
take care of this," he concludes and as the light
snaps back on the bankers and businessmen grunt
in numerous languages, jot
"take care" on their pads, smile
wanly, clap
discreetly, then promptly
forget.

(*Hans rosor är rotade i hans fotsulor.*)

Still rational and still
resolute, Mr. Lindgren sums up his speech later that night,
at a cocktail party at the Embassy.
The Ambassador listens politely, smiles wanly,
then excuses himself discreetly.
Olle Lindgren watches the man's back as he disappears,
noting absently, it's ramrod straight, yes,
oh, yes, the man sighs and walks over to the piano player, asking,
"Do you know As Time Goes By?"

Worn and weary, he sinks
into a nearby chair hoping
his favorite song will erase the day.
Hearts full of passion and hate,
the fundamental things, do they apply?
Does the world always welcome lovers?

I wonder.

I wish I were home now, yes, oh, yes, he sighs.

Hans rosor är rotade i hans fotsulor.
His roses are rooted in the soles of his feet.

III

Worn and weary after airport hustle-bustle, airport
hurley-burley, home at last but still
one more task, must take care of that report,
have it on the president's desk first thing in the morning.

Bent over his own desk, Olle scrapes pen on paper
like a hoe on unyielding soil.
He moves from sentence to sentence like a gardener.
Pruning, snipping, waiting for just the right word ...
restless, he plods from study to living room
to kitchen, where he makes himself a cup of tea.
Sipping it, smiling, yes, oh, yes, the right sentence rises
in his head like steam. He jots it down
but the next doesn't come, maybe
if I change position, and he lies down on the couch,
idly thumbing through his Oxford World History.

"The first slaves were women," he reads.

"The Sumerian word for 'slave' is 'woman from a foreign land.'
Amply legislated in the Code of Hammurabi,
the Code of Justinian and the Bible,

the nature of slavery changed with the shift
from a subsistence to a market economy.
The Turkish harem, the Roman Latifundia,
the American plantation ...
large scale demand necessitated widespread
wars and expansion of trade as slaves were seized by capture,
procured as punishment for criminal acts,
acquired as payment for debt,
secured by trade or obtained by direct sale.
Hebrew slaves baked Egyptian bricks,
Etruscan slaves baked Greek pots,
Greek slaves pulled Roman oars,
African slaves plucked Virginia cotton ..."
Olle rubs his chest as if to soothe away
the pain there, it's still the same old story, a fight
for glory, he remembers
the grunts at the conference table, the Ambassador's
armored back, why
can't I have Erik's eloquence? Why
can't I cajole, convince, connive? Why
can't I make them see? Why
don't they see?

He flips pages, muttering, "*Nu, då, nu, då.*" Now, then,
now, then, in his mind's eye Birgitta's sleeping form appears
under thousands of trodding, plodding, booted feet:
stomping across Europe for love of the spice trade,
tromping onto Portuguese ships to dare the Cape
for the spice trade, following Columbus
to America for the glory, the fundamental things, salt,
pepper, nutmeg, all is bleared with trade, smeared with toil,
nu, då, nu, even now, as I lie here, back there,
in the trade center of the world, in the financial capital
of the entire globe, in their Chinatown,
descendants of coolies stitch silk dresses
for the garment trade, in their Harlem,
descendants of field hands wipe up Burger King counters
for the fast food trade, in their Alphabet City,

descendants of peons pave the streets so that
Arabs, Turks, Egyptians, Israelis, all can walk
together, talk together, swap their goods together for cash.

Olle remembers Erik's debut article in the Quarterly Review,
The Functions of Prices in the Melting Pot.
He'd compared consumers to passengers on a steamboat,
and compared producers to the vessel's captain.
It would seem the passengers can be taken anywhere
the steamship company wishes, but really
it is the voyagers who decide
since they got on when they saw
that the boat was headed
to the place they wanted to go.

Olle gets up to pull Mikhail Gorbachev's *Perestroika*
off the bookshelf. He searches for the underlined page:
"We are all passengers aboard one ship, the Earth,
and we must not allow it to be wrecked.
There will be no second Noah's Ark."

It is so sensible.
Why don't they understand?
There is such good commercialization potential
in partnerships which could be used to finance
environmentally protective technology but salt,
pepper, nutmeg, that's
what they want.
"They shall beat their swords into ploughshares,"
said the prophet Isaiah, "and their spears into pruning hooks."
Their nuclear warheads they shall refashion
into watches and other trinkets,
thereby staking a claim to their slice of the market economy pie.
Money makes the Wall fall down,
money brings the Curtain down,
but where
is this ship
going?

Where do these passengers
want to arrive?

Olle remembers that slide he showed yesterday, earth
a shining globe aswirl
with light and shadow, so perfectly
round, so utterly
serene, and those maps,
but are they maps to a place we've already been?
And do we really want to return there?
Marathon? Hastings? Iwo Jima?
Led by some puff-chested, knock-kneed child?

Olle laughs out loud.
I just don't understand, he thinks, and while, in Sweden,
Olle Lindgren wracks his brain to write his evaluation,
in America,
six hours earlier,
the Ambassador is still asleep.
He dreams he's home, on the farm where he grew up.

Lying spread-eagled on the earth, staring up at the sky,
his body seems to be vibrating, resonating
like a tuning fork with some sound he cannot locate.
Turning his head toward the east, the dreamer sees,
at the place where earth and sky meet: a tree.
Naked, it stands with bare branches thrust up and out
as if in frenzied prayer. In four directions
around the scrawny thing there are four riverbeds.
They are filled with dust and no water.
Earth is covered with dust and no water.
Parched,
lifeless,
the sun's heat tromps and stomps with booted feet.
Earth gasps,
shudders,
shrinks.
But surrounding the tree there are thousands of women.

They are forming a huge circle.
Hands joined together, the women are dancing.
In buckskin, in togas, in sari, dashiki, bustle skirts, jeans,
brown women, black women, yellow, white, red women,
their bare feet rise and fall, pump up and down,
the rhythm of their feet rock the earth, rock life
into the earth, rock a pulse into the dying earth, in and out,
earth breathes in and out, their feet rise and fall,
the women are crying as they dance.
Their tears fall to mix with the dust of earth.
The chest of each is a bloody hole, agape,
torn veins dangle loose like roots without soil.
The women are chanting, "Mercy,
pity, peace, love, mercy,
pity, peace, love," the words echo
from the breast of earth's hills. "Mercy,
pity, peace, love," the words echo
from the folds of earth's valleys. "Mercy,
pity, peace, love," the sky
darkens, the light
turns silver. "Mercy,
pity, peace, love," earth
moans, thunder groans, clouds
swell, become turgid, stiffen in dark bulges, "Mercy,
pity, peace, love," pants earth. "Yes,"
streaks lightening. "Mercy,
pity, peace, love," shrieks earth. "Oh yes," thrusts
lightening, clouds
burst, gush forth water, life-giving water
fills the four rivers of Earth.

Entranced, the dreamer watches as, in time-lapse magic, the tree
unfolds thick green, glossy green leaves.
A voice thunders, "This Tree
will bear fruit twelve times each year,
once each month.
Its leaves will be a cure for all sickness."
Plucking one

blood-red,
heart-shaped fruit, the Ambassador
sits bolt upright in bed.
"Yes, oh yes," he mutters, "We must take care of this."
Awakened by the intercom, a sleepy secretary
plods into the Ambassador's bedroom.
"Take this telex," the Ambassador commands. "The subject is
proposed financing mechanisms for partnerships
with good commercialization potential
for environmentally benign
infrastructure investments and I want it
to go out first thing in the morning to all statesmen
and the governing bodies of the central banks
is that understood?"
"Yes, oh yes, I understand perfectly," says the secretary,
scurrying off, "I just don't understand,"
Olle repeats out loud to old Aunt Moster,
"What can I write, Hickotea?
That the trip was a total failure?"
That it's only redeeming feature was a song played on a piano at a cocktail party?"

Yes, oh, yes, Olle sighs, drifting into sleep,
the fundamental things,
as time goes by, that round globe alight, aswirl
with mercurial light, quicksilver shadow, is it a map?
No matter what the future brings,
light and shadow melt into each other, become
each other, change place, change shape, ah, they're dancing!
I knew it all along!
Moonlight and roses are never out of date.
Light and shadow meet,
greet, a kiss is still a kiss,
when two lovers woo they still say, I love you.
Light woos darkness, it is music,
darkness seduces light, it is dance ...

almost asleep now:
pulse
slow, heartbeat
steady,
a silent 'yes' on the inbreath,
a silent 'yes' on the outbreath,
balanced between waking and sleeping, yes,
poised, between light and dark, oh yes,
when winter is over.

When the snow melts and ice becomes water.

When the little bird whistles in the tree.

At the still point
of the turning world,
a glossy green tree reaches up to the sky.

And a huge round globe aslip, aslide with light and dark,
shadow etching whorls of pattern into light,
all becoming ...

light tracing petal-shaped swirls into shadow,
all becoming ...

how lovely, yes,
in the spring, oh yes,
the Rose.

Book Three

The Owl & The Stallion

THE OWL & THE STALLION

Once
upon a time or so
the legend goes once
upon a time there was a beautiful horse the horse
was big and the horse was strong and the horse
was blacker than the dark side of the moon.

No one knew where
he came from and no one
cared because if you saw him brush past
like a stroke of ink if you heard
his hoofbeats like huge
bats' wings felt
the earth quiver the wind
slice at your tongue even you
might remember things
from before you thought you could remember and jump
up from your computer or down
from your Nautilus leave
the query to flash let
the black straps hang say
"To hell with it" and run out
to join the others all of you
pointing like you've found
an oasis because it's a cool drink
of sweet water
to watch that black horse dance.

He stands there waiting proud as a Texan
sucking a cigar catching your eye he flashes

The Owl & The Stallion

like a top freezes
mid-stride like a stop-watch gallops
like a giant on a beanstalk turns
around minces
like a fairy back
to where he started and what is it

that explodes him like a grenade's pin
just snapped like tons of water
gushing from foamy heights you don't know what
to call what he's doing it's like
dancing but there's no
music it can't be
dancing but it's like
dancing so maybe
there's music
maybe
it sounds like
newborn planets crying like blind fish
discovering undersea caves like nameless flowers blooming
in unmapped forests like an ice age laughing
as it comes to an end like mountains
becoming beaches
becoming cornfields
becoming deserts
becoming glaciers then laughing
and you laugh.

You sway
back and forth.

You brush
against the fellow next to you his foot
is tapping oh-so shy then you oh-oh

give each other a sheepish grin because only fools believe
in music

Book Three

they can't
hear
so quick
wiping the smile off your face you pick up
your life like a wheelbarrow haul
your worries back
to your house climb
into your machines so when the black stallion looks up
no one's
watching

and that deep sweet well
just sprung a leak the water's seeping back
into the ground the horse
rears against the horizon like a letter in an alphabet
no one has deciphered his heart is filled
with millions of stories about millions
of beautiful things but they're written
in a language no one
understands his heart
becomes a huge eye that sees
the universe but now the eye
is filled with tears but he can't
cry if the tears get out
he'll drown so he shakes
his mane and dashes off any which-a-way to do any
which-a-thing he chases
butterflies nibbles
flowers paws
the clouds like they're grass rolls
on the grass like it's clouds pretty soon
the little forest creatures come out to get some joy
from the horse they tell the horse
their troubles the snails say
about their heavy houses on their soft
backs the woodpeckers say
about the bark tasting so bitter the squirrels say

about how the chipmunks steal their nuts
and the chipmunks say
the squirrels are bullies and the poor little ants
just work work work so the horse tries
to tell his beautiful stories but he doesn't know how
to speak snail or woodpecker he doesn't know
what words to use so he cheers them up
as best he can and runs off to be happy
the whole live-long day except when the sun goes down

the flowers
close their petals the butterflies
fold their wings the clouds
sail back to the sky the grass
sticks like glue to the earth all the little forest creatures
they go home snails
with snails squirrels
with squirrels ants
with ants they all
clump together to stay warm and safe and as the black stallion watches
evening
tucks itself
into night
like a letter tucked
in an envelope the melting sunlight
is soft wax dribbling
over the earth the horse's heart
is a huge seal he wants to press
onto the earth but what's
the use there's no one
to send the letter to so the black horse
stands still
gazing at the world with baffled
brown eyes night
gets blacker it turns into a dragon
the big strong horse becomes
a little princess in a long-ago land the sky

is a mouth the stars
are sharp teeth the princess
runs and falls and runs
and falls then she gives up she lays
on the ground sobbing because everyone left her
all alone but then she hears

the whoo-whooo
of the owl and it slays
the dragon because behind her eyes
and behind her ears
the owl takes in the world like a fish's gill takes in
water breathing in
the universe she breathes it back out
in a single bubble of a word that floats
hope
to the surface of chaos yes
it all means something yes
it all hangs together the sun and the moon and the planets
and the people it won't
all fly apart the mind
of the owl is a magnet
that pulls stray iron filings
together dense
with it all the owl
sings out a fine strong web
of a word that weaves
over the abyss so the horse is held safe
and secure

all through
the long night the world
sleeps
but the horse
listens
and knows
a new kind of joy quiet

The Owl & The Stallion

and secret like the owl a joy
that's like two halves of an oyster-shell
shut up tight
around a pearl the horse feels
precious

and only then
can he say it:

the eyes of the world
are thieves
they steal
your treasures then pawn them.
But the owl's eyes
are beggars' bowls.

And when the owl takes,
the owl keeps.

The horse feels
rich and royal but then dawn
emerges from night
like a butterfly wrestling free
of a cocoon and as morning's wings dry the owl sings
less and less until finally
the whoo-whooo isn't there
anymore
but who cares
about an old hoot owl's
silly song the black stallion switches
his tail shakes
his mane and runs off to find flowers
to nibble on.

Book Three

From deep inside
her leafy green tree the brown owl watches
with huge black eyes because the horse's prance reminds her
of a million whirling swirling things: supernovas
exploding fountains
gurgling yellow taxicabs
blurring down Fifth Avenue in the rain light bulbs
the way they flash just
before they burn out the things twirl
in the owl's mind like an alphabet
made from pinwheels the letters spell
"F-R-E-E!" the owl's feathered body
was shut up tight like a purse but now
the clasp opens and all kinds of things
spill out watching
the horse roll in the grass the owl's heavy molecules
start to zip around she starts to feel
like a helium balloon her talons
loose their grip on the branch the dragon
looses its grip on her heart because her heart
is a treasure chest filled
with jewels the owl longs
to fling them out
to the world the world
that sleeps while the owl
sings the world
that thinks the owl is just a peculiar
little brown bird with shy
ways the world whose sleep is a terrible void an airless
vacuum where the owl can't breathe but the horse
listens while the owl
sings so the dragon
can't guard her heart anymore the owl turns into
a prince who dips both his hands
into his treasure chest but just then the stallion
prances out of sight and the owl's eyes turn into
a ten-ton heart that sinks

into the ground dragging
the owl with it.

And the owl is buried
under the earth and the black horse gallops
above the earth and so it goes
for a long long time.

But flights to the moon and falling
buttons and famines and signs
on street corners and the number of peonies
in the garden this year and the ripple that schools of fish make
in the water and the number of coins
in a pocket and the number of murders
in New York City in the first half
of the second quarter of the year it's all like
a smattering of colored
glass chips.

Isn't time
like a kaleidoscope?

Doesn't it pass
as if some grinning giant
were holding it up
to some cosmic
sun?

Turning it
ever so gently then

click.

Book Three

Things seem
pretty ho-hum sometimes because that giant
twirls that tube
mighty slow it was
a ho-hum thing
to do that day autumn leaves
were scattered like jewels on a man's green
velvet lawn but what
would the neighbors think he raked them
all up he didn't care
if the ground shivered
like a dowager who couldn't hide
her naked wrinkled neck he just raked
the leaves into a nice
neat pile then set the pile
on fire and stood there watching
with a tidy little smile.

Now when fire
is inside things like stoves
and such it's like a little old lady
rocking in a chair but fire can quick
become the Wicked Queen who thinks
the whole world is her mirror mirror
on the wall she wants to see only
her very own self she wants to set it
on fire see the whole thing
flash red and wild and the wind
has a mind of its own it blows
wherever it will sometimes
it's like a kitten padding around the world
on tiny paws then
it gets huge and vicious like a Killer Whale tearing
around the sea of the world tossing
trees like ships' masts so don't

The Owl & The Stallion

you know there finally did
come a day.

And the giant was holding the world up just so.

And that tidy little fellow had his bonfire
under control.

Then the fire
peeked into her mirror the wind made
like Moby Dick flames writhed
like gypsies trees
turned into marauding bands
black smoke gathered
like limos at a funeral the forest creatures
had to run for their lives fear
wrapped around the forest like a boa constrictor it hugged
the owl it made her forget
she had wings her mind
went blank she turned cold
and hard like granite empty
like a tomb she would have died
in the fire that day except a high pitched neighing split
the air racecars
supernovas taxicabs unglued
the owl as her tree burst
into flames she flew
away then she heard it
again the black stallion was shrieking
like a derailed train pawing at the air
like an atom when the protons fall apart panicked
by the fire the horse was pulled

Book Three

in every direction at once like a merry-go-round
flying apart he would have died
in the fire that day except as he reared again he caught sight
of the owl and followed her
out of the fire.

They got
to the edge of the forest.

They meant
to part.

But when they looked
at each other the horse's heart jumped
into the owl's eyes and the owl's eyes leapt
into the horse's heart and they kept on looking
until there was nothing left
of either of them
except
the gaze
itself.

Then the owl flew north the horse followed the horse
ran south the owl followed they each took off
in separate directions except
they were together because they had fallen
into each other and fallen
through each other and fallen out
to the other side the fire
died out the wind
died away but the owl
kept flying and the horse
kept running then the owl
was running and the horse

The Owl & The Stallion

was flying then they were both
running and both
flying then there are no more words
for the way they moved the owl's wings
grew huge she was bigger
than ten horses she overshadowed
the stallion like a cloud
blotting over a hillside her wingbeats
were as loud as hooves
pounding the stallion's neigh
became soft as a bird's song
faster than the speed of light they circled the earth
seven times the horse's heart
eye merged with the owl's eye
heart blood
from the heart and tears
from the eye it all came
pouring out but the blood and the water
turned into sparks when they fell on earth the sparks became
live coals that became
seeds that became
flowers that bloomed the flowers
were alive they spoke
a new language no one
had heard before but everyone
understood it in whatever language they spoke no one
had to pluck the flowers they jumped
unbidden into peoples' hands and wove themselves
into necklaces that twined around people
two by two and when you're wearing a necklace
made from fireflowers and twined
into someone else's life it's impossible
not to giggle soon
the whole earth was filled
with giggles they got mixed up
in everything
news broadcasts, teachers'

Book Three

lesson plans chemical
formulas the giggles tickled
doctors' minds they found a cure
for AIDS the giggles grabbed
presidents' pens they signed peace treaties without knowing
why the giggles sashayed down Wall Street
there was a tickertape
parade for them the Dow Jones Industrial Average turned
into a giant Mickey Mouse balloon they let it loose
over New York Harbor and when Mickey's strings
caught the Statute of Liberty millions
of Americans watched it live
on TV, then Mickey Mouse floated off
with Lady Liberty they tracked the couple
by satellite all over the world and wherever they went
there were giggles and peace
but the owl and the stallion
still hadn't slowed down they circled the earth
seven more times
astride the horse the owl became
a King he scattered fistsfull
of jewels everywhere in Peru they found them
and bought houses for everyone in Africa they used them
to buy some rain as the King
smiled broadly the stallion turned into
a Queen decked with masses of jewels sunlight
bounced from her like a prism wherever
the beamy colors fell something beautiful
appeared in Harlem
a little boy found a bottle cap on a garbage heap and mesmerized
by its shape grew up
to be a sculptor in the biggest law firm in the world someone
was dazzled by the miracle
of a Christmas cactus and tossed out the papers
for a dishonest deal seven more times
the King and Queen passed by then
they disappeared and no one

ever saw them again
but sometimes.

If maybe one day you're feeling lost
or sad.

If maybe one day you get tired
of giving and need
to get or tired
of getting and need
to give or if you get
just
plain
tired.

If one day you're ready
to lay it all down.

If on that day you go out.

If you go out and say to yourself I'm a poor
small
weak
frightened
creature
who needs
something
and can't
get it.

Book Three

If you let yourself feel like a parking lot
with no cars like a wineglass
with no wine a ring
with no diamond and the prongs
all gaping open.

If you dare to stand there long enough
you might hear something
like an owl's whoo-whooo
dark clouds might rear up like a stallion you'll feel
wild and free and safe
and secure all at the same time you'll be in
the abyss but held
by a web you'll be so
happy you never thought
you'd ever be this happy and because this much happiness
is dreadfully sad you'll start
to cry but as the tears fall
you'll laugh because you feel heavy and light
at the same time like you're floating
off except you're anchored
to earth and the roaring
in your ears will turn
into silence from deep
within the silence you'll hear every sound
in the world as you watch
things will seem far
apart yet close
together at the same
time even things
you can't yet see and the feeling
will last for six thousand years but in about thirty seconds
it'll fade away.

You'll be left

standing there

knowing

your entire life has changed but not knowing
how or why.

You'll go home and try
to explain it to your friends but you won't
be able to because you won't know
how all those things got mixed up
together the big and the little and the wild
and the tame and the soft and the hard and the out
and the in you won't
have a word for it
but you'll want
to talk about it
so you'll call it
something maybe
you'll call it God maybe
you'll call it love you might
call it peace and cry
because there isn't enough of it you might
call it pain and cry
because there's too much of it or you'll call it
joy and write a song about it or call it
no great shakes

and shrug your shoulders
and walk away or you might think
it's so wonderful you'll make war
to get more of it kill
to defend it but no matter what
you call it or what
you do with it it's just

itself.
It's always
the same and always
different.

It doesn't need
a name because
it
is.

When you say "I am"
it pokes out from you
when I say "I am"
it pokes out
from me too there's a tickle of it
in his freckles a splash of it
on her lips it's in the dart
of a snake's tongue the opening
of a rose and there's only one way
to get it

and you already
are

and that's all
there is to it.

And it is
possible.

Even if you think
it isn't.

The Owl & The Stallion

Because once
upon a time
there were two
creatures
an owl
and a stallion.

And they found each other.

And now they just
are.

Or so the legend goes.

Book Four

Poems from the Noh

Preface

These poems began as experiments.

As I read the plays in *The Classic Noh Theater of Japan* by Ezra Pound and Ernest Fenollosa (New Directions, 1979), I began listening to the voices in the plays. The more I read – or rather, the more I listened – the more I heard something more than speech, something more than mere talking. I began hearing snatches of song. Not just in the chorus, where one would expect to hear song, but everywhere, in the middle of the plainest sentence I would hear it: music. A voice singing. Singing higher and louder than the talking, singing with the speech but also against it, part of the narrative but also somehow beyond it.

So I went through each play, underlining every phrase, line, or sentence that appealed to me as pure music. It was rhythm I was looking for. That intense rhythmic pattern of words pounding one on another: language that flows like blood, it beats so steady and so hard.

And when I was finished I went back, and saw that each fragment I'd underlined not only embodied that quality of song, but seemed to possess a meaning of its own, a meaning above and beyond its meaning in the play. The pieces I'd isolated belonged where they were when considered part of the narrative. They served their function beautifully there. But when considered separately from the dramatic action, they belonged someplace else, and seemed able to perform a very different function. It was as if each had – or wanted to have – a life independent of the life of the play, a life of its own outside the play where it could be heard and felt and understood in its own right.

For example, in the play *Kayoi Komachi*, a priest meets an old woman who refuses to tell him her name. He says:

> That's queer. I asked her her name. She won't tell me. She says she's just a woman from Ichihara, and then she's gone like a mist. If you go down by Ichihara you can hear the wind in the Susuki bushes as in the poem of Ono no Komachi's, where she says, "Ono, no I will not tell the wind my name is Ono, as long as Susuki has leaves." I dare say it is her or her spirit. I will go there the better to pray for her.

I had underlined two phrases in this passage: "gone like a mist," and "I will not tell the wind my name." Each sings. In "gone like a mist," there are two monosyllabic stressed words separated by two unstressed words. That pattern is a powerful metric unit, the English equivalent of the Greek lyric meter called 'choriambic.' Dah-da-da-dah, dah-da-da-dah, it's lovely, you could listen to it all day. "I will not tell the wind my name" is more than lovely, it's close to overwhelming with its eight single words forming four iambs. Da-dah, da-dah, da-dah, da-dah, it could pound you into the ground.

But these two phrases have something else, too. They have meaning. They resonate with implications. In the play, it's the old woman who's gone like a mist. An apt simile. But taken out of context, anything could be gone like a mist. Indeed, almost everything in our lives goes like a mist, is ephemeral, evaporates, disappears. Consequently, that small splinter, by itself, is a fact of importance to our lives. In the play, it is Ono who speaks so defiantly, who refuses to reveal her name to the wind. But "I will not tell the wind my name" bespeaks universal defiance, a defiance appropriate to any human being who feels so deeply about something that he or she will take a stand for that thing, even against nature itself.

Had I discovered, after all my underlining, that the sentence fragments represented by the two discussed above possessed nothing more than rhythm, beautiful as they were I would have proceeded no further. It was the realization that they were also significant as statements – profound statements about profound human concerns – which intrigued me. I became curious. I wanted to know what would happen if I did take them out of context and put them on their own. I wondered if the snatches of singing I'd heard could be put together to make a whole, with the music and meaning combining to make a powerful song. Since these extracts seemed to want a life independent of the plays, I wondered what would happen if I set them free.

I decided to conduct an experiment. I had my hypothesis. And I set up controls. I decided that for each play, I would pull out the phrases that appealed to me and write them down. But I imposed two limits on myself. I could make no change in the order of the words, even where I felt a slight change in wording would be better. And I had to write down the lines in the exact order in which they appeared. I started at the beginning of each play and copied down each group of words I liked until I reached the end.

The results were exciting. For each play, the bits and pieces I had culled had an incredible internal coherence when seen written out together – incredible, considering I had done nothing but rip apart whole cloth and throw a few shreds down. There was still something missing, though. I could see a real potential for power and beauty and unity in what was there on the page, but I saw, too, that this potential needed work to be fully realized. And that was where the poet took over from the scientist. I had conducted my experiment. The result was a lucky accident: bread mold. Now I had to discover the poetic equivalent of penicillin.

I went to work to make poems. I moved words around within a line, I dropped some words, I added a few of my own. I moved the fragments around, so that words which might have been at the end of a play would be at the beginning of the poem. I changed phrases into sentences, and sentences into phrases. I added and subtracted punctuation. I used parenthetical comments to function within the scaled-down framework of the poems the way the chorus functions to comment on the dramatic action in the larger framework of the plays. But I didn't necessarily put in parenthesis words from the plays' chorus. I had no intention of preserving the original meaning of the plays. I wanted to give this material the chance to shape itself into whatever it wanted to be. I wanted to give it the world of the page where it could live as a poem quite differently than it had lived in the world of the plays. I wanted to make poems that would stand completely on their own. So I tinkered to my heart's content.

Poems from the Noh

Pound and Fenollosa created with these plays objects of great beauty. One might compare them to ornate, lavish crowns. What I did was to take from each crown a jewel which particularly appealed to me, and make for it a special setting where it could be shown to its best advantage. Each poem is titled after the play from which it was taken. The reader will notice there are many poems with the same title. That's because there were some crowns from which I couldn't resist stealing more than one jewel.

E.A.

New York City
June 1978

KINUTA (I)

Sorrow!
Sorrow is in the twigs of the duck's nest,
and in the fishes held apart
in the waves.
I do not forget to weep:
my tears are a rain in the silence.

    (Upon what shall she lean tomorrow?)

What strange thing takes the forms of sound?
I have seen
what curious birds brought through utter solitude,
and hoped I might ease my heart.

    (Perhaps the moon will not call her, saying,
    "Whose nightworld is this?"
    The stag's voice has bent her heart towards sorrow.)

The last leaf falls without witness.
There is an awe in the shadow.
My blind soul hangs
like a curtain.

    (The flower lies open to the wind.
    The gazers pass on to madness.)

This flower-heart
is blown
by a wind-life
madness.

KAYOI KAMACHI (I)

I'm just a woman who lives
in all that wild grass.

>   *(She's gone like a mist.*
>   *You can hear the wind in the bushes*
>   *as in the poem where she says,*
>   *"No, I will not tell the wind my name.")*

KUMASAKA

Where shall I rest, wandering weary of the world?
They say that prayer can be heard
for even the grass and the plants, for even the sand
and the soil.
I think of these matters and know little
of anything else.
It is from my own heart that I am lost, wandering.
But if I begin talking, I shall keep on talking
until dawn.

There are winds in the east and south.
The clouds are not calm in the west.
In the north the wind of the dark evening blusters.
The moon will not break up the shadows.

> *(And so saying, he disappeared
> among the shades of the pine trees.
> And night fell.)*

SOTOBA KOMACHI

When I was young I had pride.
And the flowers in my hair.
I spoke like nightingales.

   (In its time, in its time.)

I am a stump, and well buried, with a flower
at my heart.
I am the ruins
of the daughter of my mother.

   (Over the husk of her shoulders.
   The color on distant mountains.
   A dull moon that fades in the dawn's grip.)

In the old days my lover came to me
in the dark night,
and in the nights flooded with rain,
and in the black face of the wind,
and in the wild swish of snow.

And his ghost is about me, driving me on
with the madness.

SHOJO

I dreamed a strange dream.

I waited for him where the river runs out.
Clipping chrysanthemum petals I waited for him
before moonrise.
"This is chrysanthemum water.
Give me the cup.
I take it and look at a friend."

The voice sounds clear through the shore winds.

The moon fades out of the river
and weighs down my blood.

And I am shaking and falling.

Poems from the Noh

KAYOI KAMACHI (II)

You move in ill hours.
You who left me alone, I,
diving in the black rivers of hell.
Will soft prayers comfort you
in your quiet heaven, you
who know I'm alone
in that wild desolate place?

   (Such deep thirst.)

It was not such a dark way by moonlight.
That devil in your rain was my invisible terror.
I had my own rain of tears.
The twilight was always my terror.

She will wait for the moon, I said,
but she will never wait for me.

   (It is less than nothing.)

Though she only asks me to drink a cup of moonlight,
I will not take it.

Book Four

Hagomoro (I)

Take hands
against the wind,
for it presses the clouds and the sea.

SUMA GENJI (I)

I fish in the twilight.

At twenty-five I came,
knowing all sorrow of seafare,
having none to attend my dreams.

    *(If you wait for the moonlight
    you might see it all in a mist.)*

I sing of the moon in this shadow.
I dance the blue dance of the sea waves.

    *(The waves are filled with music.
    The dream overlaps with the real.)*

My name is known to the world.
Here by the white waves was my dwelling.

    *(The wind is abated.
    A thin cloud clings to the clear-blow sky.)*

KINUTA (II)

I travel with the day.
I do not know the dreams upon the road,
I do not know the number of dreams that gather
for one night's pillow.

> *(Beware you not lose the sound*
> *of the traveling storm*
> *that travels*
> *after your travels.)*

Niskikigi (I)

There's a cold feel in the autumn.
Night comes ...
and storms. Trees
giving up their leaf.

The perpetual shadow is lonely
the mountain shadow is lying alone.
The owl cries out from the ivies
that drag their weight on the pine.

TAMURA

(It is an hour outweighing much silver.)

If you want to discover my name,
you must watch what road I take.
You must see to what I return.

(We cannot know the far or near of his route.)

I go into the mountains.

*(A man appears, lit up by the light of the flowers.
Then a shaking of mountains.)*

Look to the sea! The evil spirits
rain their black clouds. They pour down
fires of iron.
They are piled like mountains.
They fall in a swirl of hail.
The spirits are dead from the rain.

Poems from the Noh

KINUTA (III)

*(The time of regret comes not before the deed.
This we have heard
from the eight thousand shadows.)*

Aoi! for fate, fading, alas, and unformed ...
Gone from the light of the plum flowers ...
And who had not fallen
into desire? It was easy,
in the rising and falling of the smoke and fire of thought,
to sink so deep in desires.

(Tears fall and turn into flame.)

Awoi No Uye

I lie all night looking
at the moon
for sorrow.
I would not be seen by the moon, yet,
I had the moon for a mirror.

    (And the world is plowed with sorrow
    as a field is furrowed with oxen.)

NISKIKIGI (II)

Tangled, we are tangled.
We do not know where are today our tears
in this eternal wilderness.
We neither wake nor sleep,
passing our nights in sorrow,
which is in the end a vision.

What are scenes of spring to us?
This thinking in sleep of someone
who has no thought of you?
Is it more than a dream?

In our hearts there is much and in our bodies
nothing, and we do nothing at all.

Only the waters of the river of tears
flow quickly.

Chorio

A fine stork, a black stork,
sings.

The sand monkeys
cry out at midnight.

A dragon moves
in darkness.

KAKITSUBATA

Every night is a new bed, the old urge
of sorrow within me.

> *(Time does not stop, and spring
> passes.)*

I am clothed in memory.

> *(The world's glory is only for once,
> comes once, and soon fades.)*

The body unravels its shred.

> *(Thus runs each tale from its beginning.)*

What is that
that cries from the tree?

> *(It is only the cracked husk of the locust.)*

NISKIKIGI (III)

To dream under dream we return ...

    (A dream bridge over wild grass.)

You should know better than we how much is illusion.
We have been in the whirl of those who are fading.
It is for you, traveler,
to say how much is illusion.

    (Let it be a dream or a vision –
    only show me the old times
    past and snowed under.)

And you've but a moon for a lantern!
We ask you, do not wake.
You tread the border and nothing awaits you:
today's wind moves in the pines.
a wild place, unlit, and unfilled.

Poems from the Noh

NISKIKIGI (IV)

Now I have set my mind
to go as far as earth goes.

And why shouldn't I?

TSUNEMASA (I)

Bring out what stringed lutes you possess,
and I will lead you unseen:

the bass strings are something like rain.
The small strings talk like a whisper.
The deep string is the wind-voice of autumn.
The third and fourth strings are like the stork crying
in her cage when she thinks of her young birds
towards nightfall.

(And the phoenix came out from the cloud.)

SUMA GENJI (II)

The air is alive with flute sounds.
The land is a-quiver.
The wild sea is filled with quiet.

> *(Moving in clouds and in rain,*
> *the dream overlaps with the real.)*

KAGEKIYO (I)

Whom shall I ask, and how answer?
Where does the exile live?
Noise! Noise!
Ten thousand things rise in a dream, and I wake,
a nothing in the wide world.

KAGEKIYO (II)

I wear out the end of my years.
I do not know
how the time passes.
My body is but a framework of bones.
There is no one to pity me now.

    (The wind blows from an unknown past,
    and spreads our doubts through the world.)

The wind blows, and I have no rest,
nor any place to find quiet.

Genjo

The Nightingale nests in the plum tree,
but what will she do with the wind?

> *(Let the nightingale
> keep to her flowers.)*

HAGOMORO (II)

The spring mist is widespread abroad.

    (Perhaps the wild flower will blossom
    in the infinitely unreachable moon.)

Not sky is here, but the beauty,
and even now comes
the heavenly, wonderful wind!

    (It is quiet along the shore.)

There is only a fence of jewels
between the earth and the sky.

    (This alone intervenes.)

TSUNEMASA (II)

(He looked back upon the world.
His voice was heard, but none
might see him.
He looked out from his phantom,
a dream that gazed on our world.)

The figure was there and is gone,
only a thin sound remains.

(The film of a dream, perhaps.)

The rain walks with heavy feet.
They shake the grass and the trees.

(It was not the rain's feet. Look yonder.)

A moon hangs clear on the pine bough.
The wind rustles as if flurried with rain.

(It is an jour of magic.
Let no one announce the dawn.)

The sorrow of the heart is a spreading of quick fire.
The flames are turned to thick rain.
The red wave of blood rose in fire ...

(...and now he burns with that flame.)

Book Five

Songs from Silence

Eucharist

Crucified, My ribs felt like brass bands
strapping a swollen cask. Pinned
at the feet, My legs made
a goblet's stem. The words came out, "I thirst,"
but the wanting
was to be your wine.

You have always been My only desire.
I could have you if
I let you go and then flung Myself
into the space between us. In that empty air I danced
for three hours, lungs bursting
with breath I could take in
but not let out. Chest bulging,
like risen dough death kneaded me
into your bread.

Nails, nerves, lungs –
such friends, they were. With their help
I could slip secretly into your unlocked back door, disguised
as your food and drink. Like a song
filling a room I expand
to fill you, whispering,
"Open wider, little room, be
a house ...
a continent ...
the universe ...
God ...."

I grow you like bread
grows your body. I enter you
like wine,

Songs from Silence

warm, warmer until
soft as melting wax you whisper,
"Deeper." And
I Am.

Baptism

Lord, like a lily You bloom.
Roots dug deep in the dirt of me You trumpet Your perfume
through me: it's Your Love, Lord,
that fills this room.

Dust clot together makes dirt.
In the seed, life comes to be.
Water seeps down deep.
As new life unfurls earth's molecules curl tight
and cling.

Dust clot together made me.
In You, Lord, my life came to be.
With Water Your Spirit came down
to me and as Your Life unfurls my molecules curl tight
and cling.

It's Your Love, Lord, that fills this room.
Petals unfold like wings. In my chest,
heart-muscle twists like twigs in a nest.

Who knows how she knows but when
the dove knows she plucks stray bits of stuff
from the world to make for herself
a nest, a place
in the world for new life
for the world which she bodies forth
from herself.

Songs from Silence

Out of stray bits of stuff, Lord, You made me.
Made a place for me in the world then made me
a place for Yourself. With Baptism You bodied forth
Your very own Life in my very own
body and Your Life
is for the world.

It's Your Love, Lord, that fills this room.
Wings quiver like waves of light
in the night of me.

In the beginning it was dark.
Dust did clot, stray molecules
did curl, water
did cling to everything. The Spirit of God moved
over the face of the water and when God said,
"Let there be light," life
bodied forth from God's Word.
As our world unfurled God made an image
of God, a place in the world
for God's very own Life, and this Life
was the Light for us all.

God said, "Yes, this is all very good." In our breasts
choices did twist like twigs in a nest.
Life
or death. No
or yes. When we said, "No,"
death clot together in our chests, and it was dark again.

It's Your Love, Lord, that saved us. Your Spirit moved
over the face of a woman, and when she said, "Yes,
let it be done as You say," Your Word
took Its place in her womb. Your Life
unfurled in flesh. Your Light

bodied forth in the darkness.
It's Your Love, Lord, Who lived among us.
Walked with us, talked with us,
worked and slept and ate with us, then said, "Yes"
to death for us and took His place
in a tomb. After three days Your Light
unfurled in His flesh, He bodied forth
from the darkness and this new Life
was the Light for us all. In Baptism water clings
to us, Your Spirit moves
through us, Your Word
takes Its place within us and it's Your Love, Lord,
that fills this world. Bathed in it like lilies
we bloom, and it's Your Life, Lord,
that fills this world. A-quiver with it like doves we rise
up to the Light on extended wings.

PASSING THROUGH
for John King, S.J.

While ships sail for harbor –
and passengers for hearth and home –
the channel remains what it was meant to be:
a point of passage.
Marked by buoys it offers itself
to the traveler and rejoices to be nothing more than
the way.

Jesus said,
"I am the Way."
And was lifted up.
From hands and feet blood flowed freely,
and from the pierced side,
water, and welling up into many lives there beckoned
a channel, passing wayfarers safely through
to harbor.
Hearth.
Home.

Dear friend,
I have watched you move through people's lives like water.
And offer yourself to their journey.
And smile.
And let them go their way.
Your hands and feet bob like buoys,
marking the outer limits
of something which can only be known
by its depth,
and by its free flow.

Book Five

You, too, are passing through.
And so it is your God Who speaks:
"Come then, my love, my lovely one, come.
The cooing of the turtledove is heard in our land.
The fig tree is forming its first fig,
and the flowering vine smells sweet.
Come then, my dove, my little one,
out from the rocks where you've hidden,
show me your face,
let me hear your voice,
for your voice is sweet,
and your face beautiful,
and I am waiting.
And I am Home for you."

LEARNING TO LIVE AS ONE
for Charlotte & Charlie Rapisarda

Bodies are boundaries, aren't they? Hands. Feet. Skin.
We use these to mark out a scrap of territory called "me,"
then squat in it, poised
for war. On the alert
to defend. Ready
to conquer. Watching from behind our eyes
for the false move on a neighboring front which gives us
the chance to put an end to an uneasy truce.

It sometimes seems
that even smiles are a kind of plunder, booty
we cart away, shouting, "I
was there and I
won."

But "Peace I leave with you," Jesus said. "My peace
I give to you. Not as the world gives
do I give peace," and Jesus meant ...
friends, living with you I have discovered
what true peace means:

that bodies are illusions,
as laughable as a toy globe which,
with its bright colors and black lines pretends
to be the world.

That what we call "me," call "you" –
this needs to collapse so that
in the rubble of what was
what will be
can.

That peace is all the human heart yearns for:
to finish with boundaries,
to be quit of what separates,
to go beyond what divides and finally

that peace is God, and God
is our each and only Me, watching
from behind our eyes.

GRAVE-SONG
for Jesus, on Good Friday

*"Whatever came to be in Him found Life,
Life that was the Light for all."*

I

Who can sing now but the stone?

Who can have music, who can have words, the Music,
the Word,
is gone.
Who can sing now but the stone?
And the stone says,
"There is something inside me, something that shines, something
I can't reach."

The stone groaned when it closed.

II

The woman groans.
She clutches her belly in labor and thinks,
"Something! Something inside me!
Something I can't reach!"

III

Why?

Why did you take me?

Take me as if out of stone and make me
Your image?
Why did You make me new,
make me open and empty then lay Yourself in Light
in flesh
that groans, "There is something,
something inside me that shines, something
I can't reach."

The whole world sings with the stone.
And the world-song echoes from stone to stone.

IV

Our song is for You, dear Lord.
The whole world is wrapped in its song like a shroud,
we are buried with You in our own
moaning we wait, hope
like fingers that clutch,
we wait.

Lord Jesus, our Light, our Life –

Come!

FIRE FLOWERS
to the Holy Trinity, on Pentecost

Give me Your tongue to tell You, Lord,
that Your Love grows in us like red
fire flowers and when words
bloom tongues
blaze.

They waited.
They waited in a room in Jerusalem.
They were men and women waiting
for You to come to them as You had promised You would
before You left them. They did not know how
or when and the room became
a desert, with days piling up like sand that shimmered
in the heat of how, of when, until
they were prickly with waiting, like cactus, and their hearts
were all dried up.

On the tenth day You came.
The Wind they heard was Your breath, Lord,
and when their hearts burst like ripe seed pods
they saw slivers of fire
for spoors. Words
bloomed. Tongues
blazed. Three thousand came to believe that day.

Lord, I believe this whole wide world is Your garden.
Although the years pile up like sand ...
although some drop in the heat of how and when ...
although we are prickly with waiting for You, my God ...
Your Word blazes from heart to heart,
takes root, begins
to grow.

FOR RICHARD, ON GRADUATION DAY

There will be lines:
the procession.
The long waiting for your name to be called.
Then another line. One by one you will walk
up to meet someone waiting to greet you,
to give you something you have wanted.
Then back. And the line out as,
one by one you pass through into
much joy and broad smiles.

But there will come a day, Richard, later.
Maybe much later or maybe
it will come soon but there will
come a day when you will find yourself plucked
up from the line which began so clearly
here, and ended so clearly
there, with the one ahead of you, gone,
and the one behind you, yet to come.
You will find yourself hanging
in a solitary and an anguished moment, waiting
for your name to be called because someone
has something for you but you do not know who
or what or why.

On that day, Richard, I would have you remember
One Who was plucked
up and hung
on a Cross.
In a solitary and an anguished waiting He cried,
"My God, my God, why
have You forsaken me?"

Songs from Silence

Remember Him, Richard, because
He said to His God, "Into Your hands
I commend My spirit."

It is into God's hands I commend you now.
On each of your graduation days,
may you pass through into
much joy and broad smiles.

God Speaks from Within Your Heart

I. The Mother, The Father: The Only Begetter

Because I am the question to which you
are the answer I am
asking you now, "Shall we
dance?" Each time we move it is
another word in a language we are both
learning. Enfolded in Mine your meaning
unfolds, and soon
we are speaking each other.

II. The Daughter, The Son: The Only Begotten

Quarrelsome, boastful, lying, unfaithful, bound
one day to be dying you are
lodged in My heart like a grain of sand.
Layer after layer the milk of Me mothers you
into pearl.

They split My side as if shucking an oyster.
You
I give to the Begetter.

III. The Feminine, The Masculine: The Holy Spirit

Love on the wing is a bird. Are you listening?
When Love flies
you say,
"Bird." When Love swims

Songs from Silence

you say,
"Fish." When Love puts down deep roots and grows tall
you say, "Tree," and when it walks and talks
you say, "Person,"
but I say ...

won't you let
Me
speak?

You are all partners, and this dance
tells a story.
The same story.
The only story.
A story
no one has ever heard before, wouldn't you like
to listen?

The woman watching the bird, the man
catching the fish, the little child
climbing the tree ...

But you can dance or not,
as you choose. Stand,
if you want,
before another human being and refuse
to be a question. Stand,
if you want,
before another human being and refuse
to answer. Or,
if you want, you can
move. You can reach across the depths of the other's being
the way a star's light reaches across space. Where
do those beams go? They go
to you
who say, "Life."
And to you,

Book Five

who say, "Light."
And to you,
who say, "Love." And I say,

There is just
one
pearl.

Book Six

Beckonings

Book Six

Behind the walls of my eyes,
below the wells which are my ears,
beyond touch, taste and smell,
my God waits
for me.

One by one they vanish:
walls crumble, wells collapse.
Senses fail and I am here, my Lord,
with You,
my only delight.

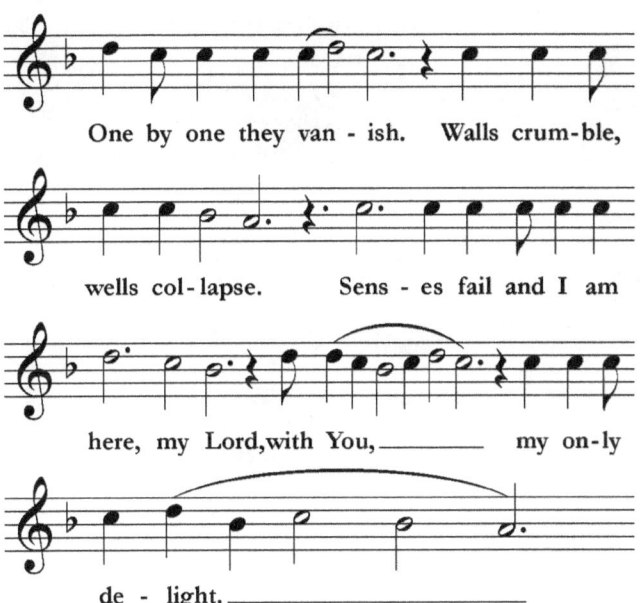

Book Six

Here is where words lose their meaning.
But, like the smile of a Cheshire cat,
one word lingers:
The Spirit and the Bride say,
"Come."

And if you wanted to remember,
after you had entered.
After you had touched and tasted and smelled the Beyond,
heard the Behind,
seen the Below ...
What one word could capture, enflesh, embody?
What one word? Only the One, True Word:
Jesus.

And If You

The Word became Flesh.
And the Word became Bread.
And the Word
feeds us, is enfleshed, embodied in you and me.
Finite, we have captured the Infinite.
And been, ourselves, caught up into the We beyond us:
the Blessed Trinity.

Book Six

Oh Lady, most pure,
Virgin Mother of God,
caught were you when the Holy Spirit overshadowed you.
You showed us the way behind,
following you we went below,
you took us all beyond
when the Word took our flesh in your womb.

Book Six

Sunlight and shadow divide the world.
And each is beautiful in its own way.
Light nudges and moves what it touches.
And darkness holds, enfolds.
They are separate yet they belong together.
We know this because diamonds are formed from coal.
My God, You hold us all together.

Book Six

Lord, I have no other desire
than to live always in Your Presence.
For You are seed and tree and root and branch;
and yet I, too, am all these things
because I am a part of You.
When I say, "I love You," this is what I mean:
that I know myself to be from You and toward You,
by You and for You ...
Lord my God, Love is forever.

Book Seven

Psalms for a New Millennium

PSALM 151

A question mark like a fish hook:
who are you, God?

As if I could catch you, wriggling
on my line.

As if I could haul you up
out of the depths of me.

Deprived of that nether atmosphere
would you gasp?
Die in my hands?

Ah, then, you must need me
as much as I need you.

Psalm 152

A parking lot with no cars.
A wine glass with no wine.
A ring with no diamond and the prongs
all gaping open ... God, my only hope
is that emptiness attracts you.

Book Seven

Psalm 153

Let's say I could put on a robe
as delicate as the petals of a flower.
A Morning Glory, let's say.
I would climb and cling.
Grow and climb and cling.
Bloom and grow and climb and cling
for and by and toward and on you,
God of my morning, forever glory.

PSALM 154

Beloved, in the hour of prayer
together we explore
the aerodynamics of grace.
You supply the wings.
I bring all the rest.

Book Seven

Psalm 155

Gaze unfocused
is the best way
to see you.

PSALM 156

You have betrayed me, God.
My rock? Quicksand
is more like it.

I no sooner get through one morass
than I fall into some fresh quagmire.
Sinking, I call out to you but
just when I need you the most,
you're gone.

Go ahead.
Say it isn't so.
Perform some divine sleight-of-hand
that proves you're there
when you're not.

What?
No answer?
It's just as I thought, you're a coward.
Quick to take credit for the good.
Never there when the blame is passed around.

Come on, Lover, fess up.
All these wars? Natural disasters?
Global warming, economic collapse,
it's all just
our free will, it's got nothing to do
with you?

We're tired of that argument, God.
It doesn't work anymore.
Too much water under the bridge, the bridge

has collapsed.
Build us another.
Or better yet, come down
to every stranded man, grieving woman,
abandoned child.
Carry us one by one to safety, to
the other side.
One by one.
Receive your praise the hard way.
Work for it.

Psalm 157

Fragile as a soap bubble,
and just as unpredictable.
My life.
Made new every day
when you sigh.

Psalm 158

When my own mother looked at me
as though I were a cockroach,
I saw myself human
in your eyes.

After my father died,
my heart shriveled like a raisin.
Your embrace
made it plump and pumping
once again.

While others may struggle to name you,
I know who and what you are.
Doctor and medicine.
Healer and poultice.
Nurse, and a comforting word.

Psalm 159

Sometimes, I fear you're gone.
But then I remember,
you're not like a button that can fall off.
Not like a key I can misplace.

Psalm 160

No mother, no father,
no sister, no brother,
no husband, no child.
Some say God is Love, but
you couldn't prove it by me.

No mother, no father,
no sister, no brother,
no husband, no child.
Some say you're a jealous God.
You've certainly eliminated the competition
from my life.

No mother, no father,
no sister, no brother,
no husband, no child: a pool
of nothingness.

But at least I know,
if I dive in after you,
I won't hit bottom anytime soon.

Psalm 161

Blessed be God.
Blessed be her holy name.
Blessed be her holy darkness.
Blessed be her holy silence.
Blessed be the mystery
in which she wraps herself.
Blessed be the inspiration
by which she shares herself.
Blessed be God in her holy creatures.
Blessed be God in her holy creation.

Book Eight

Moments Out of Time

Book Eight

THE MINDFULNESS BELL

This morning, in the meditation bell (which
I left overnight near
an open screen): rainwater, a drowned
spider, sunlight
      filling
        half the bowl while half
remains in shadow.

Why, then, sit
in silence, if everything's
already been said?

LITTLE BLIND BIRD

Little blind bird (well,
almost – still able to see
something, still able to
       flutter
near feeder, fencepost, tree limb until
the nature of the destination reveals itself and you can
       alight) – little
blind bird (plucked bald
at the neck by those who find your groping
       strange, perhaps, or
       terrifying) – little
blind bird, when you landed
on my outstretched hand: a little courage
for the blurry road
       ahead.

The Dream of Spiders

If spiders
    sleep, if they
        dream, if they yearn
            to be free of the foregone
conclusion (the web's
    sticky threads, its
        limiting boundaries, its
            mundane burden of constant repair) then
they must dream of the hunt: to stalk
    like the lion, to glide
        like the hawk, to crawl, even,
            like the snake but not
to walk about like those humans, forever caught
    in their sticky
        webs.

THE GIFT

I assumed (not
being much of a cook, never
having seen them outside the can, fresh
off the vine, gift
from a gardener friend) — I assumed
the black-eyed peas were string beans, steamed them
in their pods:
        chew,
        swallow,
        grimace,
        choke, thinking,
"I must tell Joe, his beans are tough and bitter."

        Later,
realizing my mistake, I re-examined all
my assumptions.

POSSIBILITIES

                      Pink
Mandevilla (75% off
at Lowes' end-of-season sale: glossy
        green leaves, fat
        flowers, long
          thin vines that twist, twine)
                      heaped
in a jumble on my deck as I
try to decide: you want
to climb, but indoors this winter the stakes you need will ruin
my view. I twist
future possibilities, twine them
around in my mind while yellow butterflies
                                explore
your capacious blooms, oblivious
to winter's coming, their
impending demise.

WATER SKIES

If he'd asked me (but
he doesn't know I exist) I would have advised against
the deep water start. Much easier
to begin on shore, backs
planted on firm sand, fronts
tipped up into the waves, the thrust
                  of the boat, tug
                  of the line, waver
                  between sea and land then stand
                  on water, fly
                  across it at the same time.

Now the fool is out there, trying
to keep his skies above water, nothing but water
underneath him, a beginner,
obviously, unlikely to
stand, much less
                  fly.

Seed Heads

Black-Eyed Susans withering
on your stalks
                (letting go
                of all you know: yellow
                exuberance become just
                black
                eyes)
    what can you see
                now
    that you never saw
                before?

THE AMISH WOMAN AT WAL-MART

The Amish woman at Wal-Mart
    (buggy parked
        out back in a
            truck-sized slot)
stares at her cart heaped high
with bags of potato chips. She
    (wide
        black bonnet, long
            black dress, thick
                black stockings, heavy
                    black shoes)
thinks, *I could make ten times this much for half the price*
    (hard-packed dirt, hot
        stove, thick
            grease, black
                smoke smothering
                    her dreams)
but I walk away before
she makes up her mind.

WHILE I WAIT

Flesh-eating dryer in the Ladies
Room saves
      trees, eliminates
      waste, maintains
      cleaner facilities.
I savor
the deafening noise, use my time to imagine a quiet
grave, flesh
disappeared from these bones moldering
      in a greener,
      song-filled
      Earth.

WISDOM

Serena the spider (yes,
      I've named her, how
        not?) catches flies
outside my window, hanging
by invisible threads, waiting
for something to land in her web then:
            sting,
            wrap,
            eat, quick
as a yellow wink.

            I've grown fond
of Serena and am tempted to apply
my superior skills (mobility,
      opposable
           thumbs, a fly-
                swatter) to the task of feeding her but
slowly
I catch
on.

A Contemplative's Lexicon

            Earth's
hard crust:
    silence.
            Earth's
viscous mantle:
    solitude.
            Earth's
molten core:
    communion:
    a fiery melting of all in All.

Discovery

                        White orchid

($5.99 at Food Lion, stuffed
in my cart between frozen
peas and organic
granola)

                        also called *Dendrobium*

(from the Greek:
    dendron, tree,
    bios, life,
    meaning 'one who lives
    on trees')

                        also called Hawaiian lei flower

(*nā lei*, wreaths symbolizing;
    affection, bon
    voyage, welcome)

                        found in myriad habitats

(Himalayan
    mountains,
Australian
    deserts
Brazilian
    rainforests)

                        a moment's
                        whim, an impulse
                        purchase, or

(such pilgrim
names, exotic
homelands, wayfaring
roots climbing out
of a too-small pot)

                        an invitation?

Illumination

                            I wanted
to remain in prayer,
                            I wanted
to watch sunlight
    change green leaves
        into crystal
            prisms but
                (many things seeming so pressing) I
stood up: chandelier
    shattered.

AUTUMN

How observe
    a season
        so often (and
            by so many) observed? Call

every fleeting thought a falling
    (blaze
        of scarlet? burnished
            gold? oxhide
                brown?) leaf.

Ask yourself: in
    what ground
        would such a tree
            grow?

9/11/13

                      12 years
since. Adding 1 to 2
I arrive at
3 (symbolizing a change
in present direction) then add
9 to 11 to 13 which, refined
to one digit, makes
9 (attainment, satisfaction,
achievement) then add
2 to 7 to 5 to 3, the number of people
killed, to get
8 (continuation, repetition,
cycles) then add 1 to 7 to 1 to 7 (number of families
getting no remains) to discover
7 (mystery, and, in the Bible, perfection or
forgiveness) so I stop
adding, there are too many
numbers:
        of people who lost spouses or partners
                (1,609)
        of children who lost a parent
                (3,051)
        of nations whose citizens were killed
                (115)
and I wonder
        (50 million killed
                in World War II
        70 million killed
                in the Mogul conquests
        3 million killed
                in the Crusades

will we
>   (8 billion people asking
>   the same question)

ever cease
repetitive cycles, change
our present direction, find satisfaction
in the perfect mystery of
>   forgiveness?

Sunny Morning on Herring Creek

                    White
sails (boats go back
    and forth)
                    white
gulls (birds go up
    and down)
                    white
clouds (on blue
    sky, wafting)

all drenched
    in (unmoved yet
    moving with)
                   light.

LIFE LESSON

The spider
          (day after day, pegs
          its web on a sliding
          door)
finally caught on
          (wisdom
          of experience, of trial
          and error, success
          after many failures)
tacked one
anchor thread
to the deck, now
          (perfect orb, angled
          towards the sun, aglow and
          intact as I step
          outside)
the spider
          (temperatures dropping
          in the night)
has passed on
its wisdom.

How Poetry Works

The poet blunders
into a poem like
a fly into
a spider's web. The poem

consumes her, hangs
its egg sac on fragile threads: the

delicate neurons in
some reader's
brain.

September Morning (I)

                      Red
hibiscus blossom thrusts
from green
leaves, sun-
struck.
                      Blue
sky arcs
over blue
river, sun-
dazzled.
                      Green
grass ripples
over patchy
brown earth, sun-
splashed. As

the woman gazes (sun-
suffused) she disappears
into blossoms, leaves, sky, river, grass, sun-
light, awake now, awake and

aware.

September Morning (II)

       When

the only sound is

acorns pinging from leaves
high above onto
ground below

       and

the only thought is

acorns pinging from leaves
high above onto
ground below

       then

the only word is

silence.

FLIGHT

Through convergent
evolution, different species arrive at flight
variously, so that

                                        bat wings
(membranes stretched across four elongated fingers)

                                        bird wings
(feathers attached to the fused bones of forearm, wrist, hand)

                                        insect wings
(attenuated gills of aquatic ancestors)

encourage me to believe (surrounded as I am by all this
flickering, flitting, flapping, soaring, gliding, aspiring
as I do to a lofty, airborne state) multiple
possibilities exist for

                                        human wings.

Book Eight

Dawn

like some runner
    from a far
        country arrives
            on red feet burning
with news.

CAFFEINE AND CONTEMPLATION

                      Morning
coffee in a white
cup, cup
in a
                      warming
hand, hand
                      glowing
with light, light
                      streaming
from behind.

Hand
                      holding
cup, cup
                      holding
shadows of
twig, bird, of
bird
                      alighting
on twig, a
                      living
moment complete
(like
                      living
itself) in the play
of shadow and
light.

SNIPPING FLOWERS FOR WILLIAM

(laughing monk
of Snowmass, world
traveler, God
bearer)
                          snipping

the tiny blossoms
from their fragile
stems
                          imagining

William
                          imagining

his wildflowers
arranged artfully
on a card
                          bearing

into the world a
tiny
moment
on a fragile
stem
                          blossoming

into God.

Moments Out of Time

WHEN ELLEN MEDITATES

she (according
to her letter) turns into things:

                    once, she became
                    the color turquoise

                    another time, she became
                    a lake

and one morning last week ("envision
your heart holding all the people
around you," the tape said)
                    her heart became
                    a field
people
she loved, people
she didn't know

                    all the faces became
                    flowers

in the field
of Ellen's heart

                    becoming
God

                    becoming.

Moment Out of Time

                Wind, and

multitudinous
dry leaves
                    swirling
in the crisp
autumn air.

        Behind
that veil: multitudinous
gulls
                    twirling
over a sunbright river.

        Behind
that veil: a singular
silence
                    enfolding.

Secret Birth

                      The storm clouds
parted
like the cleft
between a woman's legs.

                      The sun
crowned, flooding the world
with lusty squalls
of light.

                      The midwife
    (raindrops glistening
      multi-hued
        on green pine boughs)

trembled then
sighed.

BOOK NINE

The Raven Chronicles

Book Nine

RAVEN GAZES INTO THE FIRE

You think I can't count the cost? Me?
With these soot-black wings, this
singed song lodged
in a burnt out throat?

RAVEN FIGHTS THE WIND

Pitched against its strength, my strength
gets me nowhere.
I could give up, of course.
Turn back from this standstill mo-
ment. But then
what of the giddy slide sideways, and arriving
where I'm meant to be?

Raven Discusses Politics

I don't know why
God gave you lips and me
a beak when all you do
anyways
is stab and grab.

RAVEN THE OMNIVORE

Like you, I'll eat anything.
The world's my fridge, the door's
always open.
Kinda' lonely though.
Hard to find friends
when everything
is food.

RAVEN LONGS FOR GOD

As night's black beak closes I tuck
black bill into black wings, black tongue
still at last. I dream
I am made of salt. Fly
into the ocean, disappear.
I wake in the night, a black word melting
in God's black mouth.

RAVEN PRAISES THE COLOR BLACK

You can keep your fuchsia, turquoise,
cerulean blue.
Sunshine yellow? Hah! Cadmium red? Pooh!
I'll take black, thank you, and fly far beyond
your spectrum or science.

Raven Mourns the Start of Yet Another War

Rip
these feathers out one
by one, crush
these bones, then rejoice.
The pain
my brothers and sisters must bear, now
I can share.

Passing Over Our Lady of the Desert Monastery, Raven Shares a Thought About Discipline

Without bones, I may as well stuff pillows
with these wing feathers. Soft
is nice, but hard
gets you off the ground.

Raven Spots Ton Haak Hiking in Windmill Cove on His 60th Birthday

If he hadn't moved here of his own
free will, I'd'a gone to Holland to fetch him.
I'd'a planted tulips in rock-strewn
Windmill Cove, but
he was already at home.

RAVEN SPOUTS SOME THEOLOGY

If my eggs
were to call me Egg, they'd never hatch.
God the Father?
God the Son?
Get with the program, people –
you'll never hatch this way.

Book Nine

RAVEN COMPLAINS ABOUT LIVING HAND TO MOUTH

Well, wing to beak, actually, and it's you
complaining. Me, I'm happy with this
arrangement.
What would I do
with all that baggage?

RAVEN DESCRIBES THE HEART OF GOD

A space infinite and open, like
a baby's beak. A vast area,
enclosed, like
a nest, where all
is given, nothing
held back, all
received, nothing
rejected.

RAVEN BEARS WITNESS TO THE RESURRECTION OF JESUS CHRIST

I heard a noise, a *woomp*. It's
the sound my own wings make, displacing air
on the downbeat, sucking up
into the vacuum, *woomp*, then down
again. And then I saw something.
Someone.
Standing in the vacuum.

I've kept silent all these years, you
were just not ready.
The ball's in your court now.

Raven Becomes the Notes to a Song

I just couldn't be happy
until I took you with me.

A Message from the Author

If you enjoyed this book, please help me put it into the hands of like-minded readers. You could

- o   Write a review at your favorite online retailer.

- o   Tell you friends about it through email, Facebook or Twitter. (Or be counter-cultural – meet a friend for coffee and a nice chat.)

- o   Mention the book to fellow readers on blogs, message boards, and online forums. (Evidently, recommendations from strangers carry more weight than that of friends.)

- o   If you have a blog, please review this book.

ELIZABETH AYRES is the author of *Home After Exile, Mirror of Our Becoming, Writing the Wave* and *Swimming the River of Stone*, as well as the audiobook series *Creative Writing from A to Z* and the audiobooks in the *Invitation to Wonder 'Journey' Series,* which are based on this book. She lives in Maryland's Chesapeake Bay area, where she paces shell-strewn beaches to pluck words from the soft salt breeze.

Elizabeth holds a Master's degree in Creative Writing from Syracuse University, where she was a Cornelia Ward Fellow. She's been hailed by *New York* magazine, *New York Newsday* and the *Village Voice* for her groundbreaking teaching methods. A charismatic workshop leader for over 40 years, Ayres has taught at New York University and the College of New Rochelle; at the New York Open Center and Ghost Ranch Conference Center; through Poets-in-the-Schools and Poets & Writers; in libraries and other public forums. In 1990, she founded the Elizabeth Ayres Center for Creative Writing, which offers retreats, online workshops and private instruction to a global community of aspiring writers. Her website is www.CreativeWritingCenter.com, and you can contact her there.

THE ELIZABETH AYRES CENTER FOR CREATIVE WRITING has provided inspired instruction and supportive community to aspiring writers at every level of growth for over 25 years. The Center is both training ground and launching pad, as many published writers who got started here can affirm. The Center offers a variety of online writing classes and in-person writing retreats that will help you become the writer you dream you can be.

You belong here if

o   you sense something extraordinary within yourself and need to get it onto the page;
o   you're tired of conventional writing workshops, with their criticisms and ego trips;
o   you want a seasoned guide and affirming companions on your creative journey.

Let your creative spirit soar!

Individuals undergo personal metamorphosis as they write. Their work then helps others change. Because writers play such a critical role in our culture as it struggles to evolve, we have created a refuge where creativity takes pride of place and aspiring writers are encouraged to grow to their full potential. The Center welcomes all who wish to express themselves through the written word, no matter how little or how much experience they have.

Visit the Elizabeth Ayres Center for Creative Writing

www.CreativeWritingCenter.com

or call 1-800-510-1049

Also by Elizabeth Ayres

How often does your mirror say, "You are beautiful, you are wise, you are loved?"

Mirror of Our Becoming is a collection of 60 short reflections revealing the reality of your existence: that the beauty around you is already inside you. It will show you how to align yourself with that grand tapestry in which you're a single, essential thread. It will prove you're infinitely lovable, inexhaustibly loving, and tenderly held by love's great purpose.

Organized by season, this profoundly hopeful book will carry you through an entire year. It will give you courage in times of trouble; profound satisfaction in times of joy. In its pages, you will know a healing communion with your inmost self, with the world, and with that divine and holy mystery to which we give many names.

This volume includes a discussion guide for readers, with questions to help you, your family and your friends enjoy your own encounters with Nature more fully. There's also a study guide for aspiring writers.

We cannot see our own faces. In graceful, elegant prose, this book shows us who we are and what we can become, because the beauty, wisdom and mystery in which we dwell is the truth that dwells within us.

"Ayres' poetic vision transforms ordinary perceptions into mystic beauty."
 – Beatrice Bruteau, *The Grand Option* and *Radical Optimism*

"Lovely! Shows amazing breadth of thought!"
 – Thomas Berry, *The Great Work* and *The Universe Story* (with Brian Swimme)

"The imagery is amazing. It took me back to my own childhood—I felt as if I were there, on the beach, laughing with friends and feeling the sea breeze. To actually feel this just from reading is quite the feat."
 – MDDC Press Association

For more information or to order, visit www.CreativeWritingCenter.com/books/mirror-of-our-becoming.

Also available in audiobook form

Every reflection in *Mirror of Our Becoming* is available in audiobook form under the title *The Invitation to Wonder 'Journey' Series*. To listen to samples or place an order, visit www.CreativeWritingCenter.com/audioboooks/invitation-to-wonder-journey-series.

Also by Elizabeth Ayres

What does home mean to you?

Elizabeth Ayres begins life in an orphanage. Her adopted father dies when she's six. Her adopted mother says she's a worthless piece of garbage. Her stepfather haunts her bedroom at night. Elizabeth comes of age damaged, frequently suicidal and headed for disaster, yet, through all the darkness, a mysterious 'something more' always beckons. As a young girl, she builds altars in the woods to commune with a numinous Presence that is both More and All. As an adult, she scoffs at such childish nonsense and sets out to find more prosaic cures for the loneliness that dogs her every step. Marriage. A convent. A search for her birthmother. Still it lures her on, that tantalizing glimpse of wholeness and belonging she had savored as a child. Finally and miraculously given, in the most unlikely place of all.

"Spellbinding and beautifully written. *Home After Exile* is an archetypal story of redemption that could change the way we relate to ourselves, each other and the planet."
— Annie Dillard, *Pilgrim at Tinker Creek*

"This new book by Elizabeth Ayres is deeply moving and disturbing. It's the story of a human soul imbued with dreams, hopes, terrors, confusion, violence and deep intelligence. Ayres opens her soul to the world, revealing an insuperable human spirit that remains—despite years of abuse and abandonment—infinitely free and deeply in love with the God of life. This is a book to be read slowly and reflectively. Ayres is a poet, an artist of the human spirit, whose journey through death into life bears witness to the power of that divine Love which carries us on eagles' wings."
— Ilia Delio, OSF, *The Unbearable Wholeness of Being*

For more information or to order, visit www.CreativeWritingCenter.com/books/home-after-exile.

Also by Elizabeth Ayres

Where's *your* wave of creativity?

There's a vast ocean of inspiration within you, and you can tap into its power just by following the exercises in this book. Even if you're doubtful, intimidated, or blocked, the words soon will be surging out of your pen or keyboard, rushing onto your once-blank page like surf onto the shore.

Elizabeth's warmth and wit sparkle in every chapter. You get a personal writing coach who makes the creative process easy and fun while honoring its depth and mystery. The step-by-step instructions work for fiction, nonfiction, poetry, screenplays – anything your imagination can suggest, these exercises will bring it forth. And along the way you'll learn tools and techniques you can repeat again and again, whenever you want to write your wave.

Ready to take the plunge?

"Hands down, the best writing book on the market today."
—Annie Dillard, Pulitzer Prize-winning author of *Pilgrim at Tinker Creek*

"Elizabeth Ayres has thought long and hard about the writing process, and is one of the most seasoned and exemplary practitioners in the field of teaching writing. This book is an invaluable distillation of her insights and experiences. I cannot imagine any beginning or struggling writer not coming away with some inspiration from it."
—Phillip Lopate, editor of *The Art of Writing* and *Writing New York*

For more information or to order, visit www.CreativeWritingCenter.com/books/writing-the-wave.

Also by Elizabeth Ayres

Containing original material not published anywhere else, the audiobook series **Creative Writing from A to Z** shows you how to break through inner obstacles, unleash your imagination, and master the skills you need to become the writer you dream you can be. You'll learn

- o "Imaginative Layering," a breakthrough technique for generating limitless creative writing ideas;

- o "Extrospection," a powerful method for using your five senses to get "unstuck;"

- o "Structure," an intuitive, right-brained approach to organization that reveals the underlying shape of any fiction, nonfiction or poetry writing project.

You'll also find dozens of other exciting tools to help you overcome writer's block, take your craft to the next level, and jump start your imagination with the guidance of an exceptional teacher.

To listen to a sample or to order, visit www.CreativeWritingCenter.com/audiobooks/creative-writing-from-a-to-z.

Acknowledgements

This 'collected works' is a gathering of poems written over a lifetime, and for their enduring friendship over that span, I thank Candy Cummings, Janaki Patrik, Jane Sypher and Rhoda Neshama Waller. Candy's exuberant creativity and generosity of spirit are always an inspiration. Janaki's breadth of vision as a choreographer, her inimitable brilliance as a dancer and her dedication as a teacher have always amazed me. Neshama's spiritual depth, her passionate love of the written word and her penetrating wisdom are qualities I've always relied on. Jane's true-blue faithfulness, as well as her selfless devotion to her family and community, are models we would all do well to imitate.

For their loving presence in my life now I thank Janice Booth, Kellie Gofus, Jim Walsh, Kristan Huthmacher, Helena Clare Pittman, Karen Karper Fredette and the Franciscan Sisters of Washington, D.C. Much gratitude goes to my friend and prayer partner, Theresa Prymuszewski; to my friend, neighbor and landlady, Nancy Allwine; to Sr. Laura Smith, CSJ, for her spiritual guidance; to Jan Booth and Paul Schulkind, for copyediting assistance; to Bill Earle, the Project Manager at Accurance.com and to the entire production team at Accurance, for creative book design and efficient, courteous book production; to my cover designer, Karen Phillips of PhillipsCovers.com, for her imaginative cover designs and companionable working style; to Gabe Halberg of DadraDesign.com, for his stellar web design as well as his diligence, patience and sense of humor.

ELIZABETH AYRES is the author of three other books: *Home After Exile, Mirror of Our Becoming* and *Writing the Wave*, as well as the audiobook series *Creative Writing from A to Z* and the audiobooks in the *Invitation to Wonder 'Journey' Series*, which are based on *Mirror of Our Becoming*. She lives in Maryland's Chesapeake Bay area, where she paces shell-strewn beaches to pluck words from the soft salt breeze.

Ayres holds a Master's degree in Creative Writing from Syracuse University, where she was a Cornelia Ward Fellow. She's been hailed by *New York* magazine, *New York Newsday* and the *Village Voice* for her groundbreaking teaching methods. A charismatic workshop leader for over 40 years, Ayres has taught at New York University and the College of New Rochelle; at the New York Open Center and Ghost Ranch Conference Center; through Poets-in-the-Schools and Poets & Writers; in libraries and other public forums. In 1990, she founded the Elizabeth Ayres Center for Creative Writing, which offers retreats, online workshops and private instruction to a global community of aspiring writers.

Elizabeth Ayres can be contacted through her website: www.CreativeWritingCenter.com.

www.ingramcontent.com/pod-product-compliance
Lightning Source LLC
Chambersburg PA
CBHW020753160426

43192CB00006B/323